ICH BIN EIN JUDE

Warmest Regards!

Herb Brin

Aug 8, 1983

By the same author:

Wild Flowers
Justice Justice
Conflicts

Soon to be published:
My Spanish Years

ICH BIN EIN JUDE

Travels Through Europe
on the Edge of Savagery

by
HERB BRIN

with a Preface by
ELIE WIESEL

jɒ JONATHAN DAVID PUBLISHERS, INC.
MIDDLE VILLAGE, NEW YORK 11379

ICH BIN EIN JUDE

Jonathan David Publishers, Inc.
68-22 Eliot Avenue
Middle Village, New York 11379

Library of Congress Cataloging in Publication Data

Brin, Herb.
  Ich bin ein Jude.

  1. Jews—Poland—Addresses, essays, lectures.
2. Holocaust, Jewish (1939-1945)—Poland—Addresses,
essays, lectures. 3. Poland—Description and travel—
1945- —Addresses, essays, lectures. 4. Brin, Herb—
Addresses, essays, lectures. 5. Journalists—United
States—Biography—Addresses, essays, lectures.
6. Poland—Ethnic relations—Addresses, essays, lectures.
I. Title.
DS135.P6B75   940.53'15'03924   81-15256
ISBN 0-8246-0275-7   AACR2

          10   9   8   7   6   5   4   3   2   1

Printed in the United States of America

. . . to Children,
Children I did
not find

IN GRATITUDE

Every newsman has the compulsion to write his one "big book."

Alas, all mine are small ones, including *Ich Bin Ein Jude*. Covering the history of a people, once said, what is there to say but sigh?

I admit I had intended to present a broad canvas, but alas the painting (the book) contained its own brushmarks. I felt, watching from a distance, that this book wrote itself.

My gratitude, first, to Elie Wiesel, who encouraged me to do the book. His encouragement was heartening and inspiring. Elie is part of my life forever.

In the process, I hasten to extend gratitude to those others who, in countless ways, made possible my strange journey "on the edge of savagery."

Professor and Mrs. Abe Nasatir have been the superconsciences of all my writings, and to them my profound respects.

My three sons—Stan, David, and Dan—suffered through the original drafts and helped shape the final manuscript.

To Tom Tugend, senior associate editor of *Heritage* and my lifelong friend, gratitude for valuable assistance in clarifying the German language used in this volume. Professor Will Kramer scanned early drafts with his perceptive eyes and helped the project along.

UCLA bibliographer Shimeon Brisman was helpful in the early stages of translation of Elie Wiesel's French preface to the book, and UCLA staff librarian Rudolf E. Bart was gracious in the actual translation of the preface.

I hasten to acknowledge the cover artistry of Dorothy Orr, one of the unusual West Coast artists. Gratitude also goes to *Heritage* staffers Bertha Bernstein and Helen Saab, who helped prepare the final drafts for publication.

A word of respect to Leo Bach, whose notes on Jewish life in Krakow play an important role in the story which I tell.

Finally, special thanks to Rabbi Alfred J. Kolatch, of Jonathan David Publishers, Inc., who had the courage to take on the publication of *Ich Bin Ein Jude,* knowing the usual problems in distributing such a work.

—HERB BRIN

September 1, 1982

A Letter of Introduction
by Elie Wiesel

Cher Herb Brin:

Je suis content de vous avoir encouragé à écrire ce livre. J'espère qu'il touchera le lecteur comme il m'a touché, moi.

Qu'est-il exactement? comment le décrire? Recueil de reportages, de choses vues, rêvées et vécues, de méditations poétiques et philosophiques, de souvenirs proches et lointains: c'est une somme d'expériences juives et humaines que vous nous livrez, cher Herb Brin. Et nous vous en savons gré.

Grâce à votre vocation de journaliste, vous savez nous faire voir et sentir hommes et paysages proches et lointains. Poète, vous possédez le don de faire vibrer les mots et même de les faire chanter. Juif, vous est conscient de votre devoir de témoigner pour notre peuple.

Vos pélerinages aux sources de notre mémoire commune—au fond de l'angoisse comme au coeur de la joie—sont bouleversants; ils sont à la fois simples et obscurs, lyriques et durs. C'est la gorge serrée que le lecteur vous suit en Pologne et de là, inévitablement, à Jérusalem. Parfois vous lui parlez, mais il vous arrive également de parler à sa place.

Oui, vous avez bien fait de retourner *là-bas,* de l'autre côté de l'Histoire raisonneuse et raisonnable, pour écouter le dernier sage juif de Varsovie, pour voir les nuages qui passent au-dessus de Majdanek, pour déchiffrer les visages des êtres qui hantent vos songes.

On vous conseillé de ne pas considérer les Juifs comme s'ils étaient le "Pipik" du monde? La plaisanterie est déplacée et de mauvais goût. Nos ennemis seuls nous voient partout; on dirait qu'ils ne pensent à rien d'autre. Nous les intriguons, nous les obsédons: leur ferions-nous peur? Nous sommes leur idée fixe. Ils ne sont guère la nôtre. Notre vocation est universelle, et notre mission l'est aussi. Vous l'avez compris, vous. En parlant du fait juif, vous traitez du problème humain. Pour un Juif il serait impossible d'atteindre l'universel autrement que par son judaisme. Un Juif qui pense devoir renier son judaisme, ou même l'amojndrir, pour mieux aborder les questions géné-rales, finira par parler à côté: son discours sonnera faux.

Voilà ce que je trouve dans votre volume: un amour pas-sionné de notre peuple, et à travers lui, de tous les hommes qui sont capables et dignes de se réclamer de l'humanité.

Vous sentez le chant monter en vous, et c'est une melodie du passé lointaine qui se fera entendre; vous marchez dans les rues d'une capitale quelconque, et c'est le nom d'un prophète—Jonah? Isaie? Jérémie?—ou d'un poète—David?—qui sera prononcé; vous ouvrez les portes du passé et vos soivenirs appellent des Juifs que j'ai rencontré, moi, ailleurs, en d'autres temps, sous d'autres cieux. C'est qu'un homme comme vous, un poète comme vous, ne peut pas et ne doit pas ne pas chercher ses frères parmi les morts *et* parmi les vivants.

Certes, on vous dit: mais les autres? les Juifs n'étaient pas les seuls à souffrir, ni à périr? après tout, ils étaient onze millions à subir la mort au mains des tueurs nazis … N'écoutez pas, continuez à ne pas écouter. Poursuivez votre route. Dites-vous bien que lorsqu'un poète juif chante l'expérience et pleure la mort de ses frères, il va au-delà d'eux: c'est en les évoquant, qu'il rappelle tous ceux qui, pour d'autres raisons, ont connu leur sort. Soyons précis: si nous, Juifs, nous souviendrons de nos six millions de victimes, le monde se souviendra des autres aussi; si nous mêlerons les notres dans un vaste anonymat, toutes seront oubliées.

C'est donc contre l'oubli que vous élevez votre voix; et c'est pour illustrer la valeur du défi que votre chant retentit: ces Juifs russes que nous avons rencontré, vous et moi, ne sont-ils pas une preuve vivante que la mémoire juive—donc humaine et souveraine—ne sera jamais étouffée?

Dans ce livre, cher Herb Brin, vous avez su écouter les témoins. Or, vous le savez bien: qui écoute un témoin le devient.

ELIE WIESEL

Aseret Yemei Teshuva 5742

A Letter of Introduction
Translated from the French
by Rudolf E. Bart

Dear Herb Brin:

I am glad that I encouraged you to write this book. I hope it will move the readers as much as it has moved me.

What is it exactly? How can one characterize it? It is a collection of reports of things seen, dreamed about and experienced, poetical and philosophical meditations, memories from far and near. It is a summary of Jewish and universally human trials that you are offering us here. And we are grateful to you for them.

As a journalist, you are able to make us see people and scenery at close range and at a distance—and to get a feeling for them. As a poet you have the gift of making the very words vibrate and even of making them sing.

As a Jew, you are conscious of your duty to be a witness for our people.

Your pilgrimages to the very sources of shared memories,

to both the depths of anguish and of joy, are upsetting; they are simple and obscure, lyrical and harsh.

With a lump in the throat, we follow you into Poland and from there, inevitably, back one day to Jerusalem.

At times you are speaking to the reader; at other times you are speaking in his stead.

Yes, you have done well to return to that region beyond the cold facts of history, to let that last wise Jew of Warsaw speak out, to review those clouds that hang over Majdanek, to reveal and interpret the faces that still haunt your dreams.

Some people suggested to you that you should not see the "Pipik" of the world in the Jews. This is sheer mocking, and in bad taste at that. Our enemies claim that we are ubiquitous; it seems that they can't think of anything else. We are intriguing them, we are haunting them; are we frightening them? We are an obsession to them. They can't frighten us. Our calling is universal and such is our mission. You have grasped this truth: when you speak about the Jews, you speak of a problem that concerns all mankind. For a Jew it would be impossible to approach this universal problem otherwise than from a Jewish viewpoint. The Jew who might feel compelled to renounce his Judaism or to water it down in order to be able to speak better about universal problems would strike a wrong note; his voice would have a false ring.

This, then, is what I find in your work: a passionate love for your people, and through it, for all men who are worthy of being called humans. A song is rising out of your heart; a melody out of the remote past can be heard. When you are wandering through the streets of any capital city, the name of a prophet is on your lips—Jonah? Isaiah? Jeremiah?—or the name of a poet—David?

You open the gates of the past and your words bring back the memories of Jews I have known, somewhere, sometime, in other lands. This is so because you, as the man and poet you are, cannot but seek your brethren among both the dead and the living.

Of course, some people may ask you: and what about the others? The Jews were not the only ones to suffer and perish? After all, there were eleven million who suffered death at the hands of the Nazi killers. . . .

Don't listen to them, keep on not listening to them.

Go your way. Remind yourself that when a Jewish poet sings about Jewish trials and sorrows to the agonies of his own brethren, he includes with them all those others that have met a like fate, although for other causes.

Let's state it precisely: If we Jews commemorate our Six Million victims, the world will remember the others too. If we allow ours to be just a part of an anonymous multitude, all will be forgotten.

It is against this tendency to forget that you raise your voice. It is in order to illustrate the virtue of accepting the challenge that your song rings out: those Russian Jews we have met, you and I, are they not living evidence that the Jewish memory—and hence the human and sovereign memory—will never be snuffed out?

In your book, my dear Herb Brin, you have shown that you know how to listen to witnesses.

Now, as you know well: whoever listens to a witness becomes a witness himself.

ELIE WIESEL

Aseret Yemei Teshuva 5742
Ten Days of Repentance 1981

Ich bin ein Jude!
What the hell, I learned long, long ago on Claremont Avenue in Chicago there's no escape from what I am and if I had to slug my way through life's realities ... what the hell, indeed. Life is a matter of urgencies and choices—so of course I chose the accidents of genes of countless others before me to be born as I was. A Jew.

What makes you think your own choices are special, unique? We all sink our footprints into the sands of time and somebody comes along and kicks it all away. Or a flood floats it into the deep and another shnook comes along with big feet and thinks his footprints are forever.

Fragility. Like the wind blowing on a spent dandelion. Poof.

But that's in the course of human events. Puppies are born, they cut their teeth on bones—and as the days race along, their tails wag ever so slowly. And they sigh, like the rest of us. Life's cycle.

I am a newsman on the prowl for instant history. My vehicle: four tiny Jewish newspapers in California. I make no pretenses; I move no worlds. I observe and sometimes holler like hell.

Given memory, given history, my own genetic senses can accept the human cycle. But I can never accept the German manufacture of closure for my history. And so I have sought out some of the realities. The banalities. And have taken this journey through a Europe still reeling on the edge of savagery. Thirty-five years later.

Do you think for a moment any of it is forgotten?

Bring along your own measures of madness. Let's make it a bacchanal.

But first, I tell myself, choose a point of departure. It hardly matters where, at what point. It all led to murder.

I wasn't actually part of the banality. But did anyone on earth really escape it?

Point of departure: An awareness that I've lived an unfathomable expanse. My first transport a horse and wagon on Chicago's Northwest Side—and now my astronomer son charts the heavens. But then, our sons have been doing that since Jewish tears salted the waters of Babylon.

Between my childhood journey in Uncle Sholom's wagon to the star treks of my son, convulsions grabbed humanity by the throat, shaking away like hell. History has no parallel for it. This time, for the book, I went out to look in on it: to ask a few questions seeking gossamer answers. But, hold on to your feelings.

*   *   *

My sons insist: write it down. Elie Wiesel asks to see my material when his eyes are more penetrating than mine. He lived what I brushed against as an outsider. Nor do I have documents to fall back upon—merely an explosion of memo-

ries for unfolding chapters to a savage book that began inno-
cently enough with my first awareness of travel at about three
years of age.

Uncle Sholom had piled a few of our household items on his
small carpenter wagon, and the horse (I learned later he was the
actual horse brought over by Tevye himself—he was not?, no
matter) pulled us. Uncle Sholom, my mother, my father, my
brother and me. To Claremont Avenue. Our first flat, a basement hovel next door to the Shul, the Synagogue my father
wouldn't go to because he liked the rabbi better at the Artesian
Avenue Shul. Two blocks away.

Wouldn't the rich ones, the very richest of them on the cattle
cars to Auschwitz (the Orient Express, indeed) have given a
life's ransom to live in our basement hovel, had they known?

Choose a point of departure.

Well, then, I choose. 1962. The Mountain of Remembrance
in the Hills of Judea on the eventide of dedication of Yad
Vashem, the Forest of God's Name—the western sky aglow
with the gold and purples and silver halos about the clouds of
fleece drifting toward the east. As the world turns. And the
dedicatory address by Abba Eban, weaving words of comfort
and pride and promise that a people of history had paid its price
to history. Oh, in so many ways paid that price demanded by
history.

The great plaza outside the temple of rock that contains the
ashes of our sorrows was a sea of mankind, awed by it all. The
inheritors of Auschwitz; they were there to witness dedication
of a temple to the victims of the madness of government. In the
tender warmth of a Judean spring sunset, we listened to an
oration, the words drifting with the winds over the nearby military cemetery where lie the Jewish heroes who made possible
this return to Biblical promise.

My mind kept wandering to the Grand Diaspora: we had
come back from so many lands to these barren Judean hills
where our Prophets walked a breathless time ago—to these

hills that were denuded of life by Rome, and salted, to destroy the very earth. Two thousand years ago.

My diaspora was a tiny enclave of Chicago, about eight or ten square blocks. There was the horseradish grinder on every corner. Soapbox revolutionaries urged us to revolt. From what? To what?

Scanning horizons beyond Abba Eban, the crags of Judea tasting amber in the descending sun and the mind racing from Claremont Avenue to the *shtetlach* of Europe to the illegals fleeing leaking hulks on the shores of the Promised Land to escape the British, and the Arab, then back again to the tiny Shul on Claremont Avenue where I'd regularly be pulled inside by the *shamos* seeking his afternoon "tenth"—because no gathering in prayer may proceed without a tenth to compose a *minyan*. The *shamos* always said it was a *mitzvah* to give up baseball to be a tenth. A good deed to God. But, I was a lousy baseball player anyway. Couldn't catch a fly.

Little did the *shamos* know that when it came to prayers, even the Lord Almighty would smile. For I'd been kicked out of religious school for laughing when we came to the innocent Hebrew word *fukdainu*. Darned if other young Jewish boys didn't have their religious education truncated by that damned word. Oh, I should be smiling at it all now, for as days doth pass, beauty often followeth chagrin.

Yet, there I was, atop the Mountain of Remembrance on the plaza before the Yad Vashem, listening to one of the great orators of history recreate our Jewish passions.

The day had begun for me right there at Yad Vashem and I had been riveted to the scene by factors over which I had no control.

A halt had been called to the Eichmann trial, which I was sent to cover for the Los Angeles *Times.* I hiked the mile or so to the Yad Vashem in order to pick up some background notes for the day of dedication. Suddenly, a platoon of Jewish soldiers appeared on the plaza, emerging from somewhere deep in the

Judean Hills. These were tall, exceedingly beautiful men, stern soldiers in slow, mournful cadence.

In the center of the double column of soldiers were four, carrying a small granite coffin.

They marched in the beauty of sorrow, a brisk, slow step— carrying ashes from Auschwitz through the Hills of the Prophets—to Yad Vashem.

I followed the soldiers inside, past the iron doors fashioned after the barbed wires of infamy, into the sallow darkness of a huge cave of rocks: boulders upon boulders forming walls for an enormous concrete canopy.

The soldiers paced steadily forward to an open grave in the huge floor containing markers of all the camps that were intended by the German to end the Jewish experience on earth.

Two men were standing inside the open grave to lower the granite casket into the Judean mountain. A symbolic burial, to be sure. For how many were the bodies that formed the ashes that filled the casket? Is it not forbidden by Jewish faith to accept cremation as a conclusion of life? Indeed, how would the bones be gathered upon the day of the gathering of the bones, as it is written?

The granite casket had its own will, this day. It fell out of the hands of the soldiers and through the hands of the waiting men inside the open grave and down into the soil of Jerusalem. There was a gasp that swept witnesses to this drama. There was nothing left to do but cover the grave with its Auschwitz marker, light an eternal flame and listen to the soulful chant of the *El Mole Rachamim.*

Then, to go outside to the plaza for the sun to descend and Abba Eban to address the gathering.

One wonders what decisions had brought Abba Eban to his commitment to Israel. A master of intellect and ideas, his very breath composed a cadence of words and phrases that galvanized Jews for whom English, not Hebrew nor Yiddish, nor even French, was the *lingua franca* of my time.

But then, I knew what brought me there to the Mountain of Remembrance: I survived the German era and now bear the guilt of that survival and for what I did not do.

Do you think for a moment that the protective blocks of Jewish life near Humboldt Park in Chicago was a shield from the Abie Kabbible jokes one heard upon leaving our *shtetl* to go to the library at North and California Avenues, and thus having to go through the Polish section?

Ben Hecht went to the Schley School, then fled Downtown to the daily papers; then on to Hollywood. Saul Bellow went to the Schley School and grabbed a gold ring on the Nobel merry-go-round. Arthur Goldberg came from the neighborhood and fled to the Supreme Court and Hymie Rickover—hell, he's forever!

But they (we) all fled the shoemakers and junk dealers and horseradish grinders and the *shulkelach* just as Abba Eban fled the constrictions of a world he never made and created grace and dignity for our people when he took the rostrum at the United Nations, while brave men were dying to recreate a Jewish State, here, upon these Judean hills.

On the Day of Remembrance, all the world knew that a people of extended memories would never forget.

The eventide was embraced by lengthened shadows of twilight while tender western winds touched us with darkness.

The Eichmann Trial. Soon the equations of life would bring me back to reality. It wouldn't be long in coming.

2

Yom Hashoa, the Day of Remembrance, was followed by Independence Day—and a parade of Israel's Defense Forces, tanks and all, through the boulevards leading from the government buildings to the Hebrew University.

The tanks, of course, churned up the pavement, but the hundreds of thousands of Israelis who had come out to cheer for the home team couldn't care less. It was a lift to the morale to see Mystere jets streak across the skies of Israel in formation of a gigantic Star of David. The message was necessary to be conveyed to their troublesome neighbors. Jordan was a rifle shot away. The shells of Syria were raining down on Jewish farmers in the Galil. These facts were as real to the Israelis as the trial of Adolf Eichmann which was about to unfold at Beit Ha'am, the House of the Nation, also a rifle shot away in Jerusalem.

The issue of the day was a towering one: did the Israelis have a right to land a team of armed men inside a foreign and friendly nation, Argentina, and by ruse spirit Eichmann away to stand trial in Jerusalem before a tribunal of Jewish judges?

Many editorialists of the day declared pompously that Israel had done an injustice to the cause of justice. But then, few of them ever heard the anguish of a mother watching Germans smash her baby's skull against a wall. After all, ours was the crime of history: being born into the kinship of David.

Israelis chose not to respond to charges that they had not the right to grab an Eichmann wherever he might be found. The issue itself became moribund when evil and banality and the German nation's murderous heart were laid bare.

As luck would have it, I was assigned by the Israel Press Office to living quarters at a family pension a short distance from the Mountain of Remembrance, with its Yad Vashem and adjoining military cemetery where the highest point was given to the remains of Theodor Herzl, the Austrian journalist who dreamed the rebirth of a Jewish State at the turn of the century.

My room at the bed and breakfast pension was a tiny alcove overlooking the Hebrew University and the Knesset, Israel's remarkable parliament building. From that vantage, the Independence Day fireworks display was overwhelming. The skies were aflame with sparklers.

Here was a new breed of Jew, one that would spring phoenix-like from the ashes of tragedy. Youngsters were dancing in the streets throughout the night. This was the way it wasn't supposed to be for inheritors of Abie Kabbible, the king of the Jews.

Looking in another direction from the roof outside my alcove, I could scan distances toward Latrun, the fortress which Britain turned over to the Arabs in the 1948 War of Liberation, an action which almost throttled the rebirth of Israel. For Latrun dominated the only road to Jerusalem. And in the fields below Latrun, seeking to open the roadway to Jerusalem, hundreds of wretched Jews who had just come out of the hellholes of Poland and had boarded ship at long last to freedom, died.

As they left ship, they were handed guns and taken to the fields of Latrun. Only a few survived. They were confronted with military commands in a babble of languages. And they were hardly trained for war. Only for grief.

*   *   *

The prosecution of Adolf Eichmann was the only time a major German participant in the "Final Solution" was to be brought to trial in Israel. Indeed, anywhere.

It was at the pension in which I had been given an alcove that the entire defense staff of Eichmann had also been assigned. An uncanny accident. Several German editors were also assigned to the pension. It was inevitable for close contacts to develop at breakfast, at dinner, at brandy time. Indeed, brandy on the rocks, a thought which once sent shudders through me, emerged now as a civilized concept among a team of German lawyers in Jerusalem who were there to attempt to save the life of a master of railroad logistics.

When Dr. Robert Servatius, chief lawyer for Eichmann, raised the issue of propriety for a Jewish court to try the defendant—because all Jews must in their revulsion be preju-diced, Gideon Hausner, the prosecuting attorney, said that the test of justice is not that a jurist comes to a trial with his sorrows and personal feelings intact. "The test of justice is that the judge be fair," said Hausner.

Daily, witnesses came forward to tell of their contacts with Eichmann, who was protected from possible attack by a bullet-proof glass cage. Each described Eichmann as a meticulous craftsman who knew where every unused railroad freight car was located in German Europe. Even when the German mil-itary was hard pressed for rolling stock, the Eichmann express trains ran—from Salonika to Vienna to Poland; or from Drancy to Vienna to Poland. Most of the way on tracks of the Orient Express.

Once, prior to court, I managed for a moment to sit inside

Eichmann's glass cage. I conceived myself seated in the hottest chair in human memory. I shuddered, scratched a few notes for a report to the *Times,* then fled; hot sweat over me.

That night I sent along a single question to Adolf Eichmann through his staff to be raised by Dr. Servatius at a meeting with Eichmann in his holding cell. With the trial already weeks along, did he think he was receiving a fair trial from the Jewish court?

"Eichmann told me that he could not have received a fairer trial in Germany," said Servatius several days later. It was Eichmann's only contact with the press.

I walked out into the garden with two Servatius aides. We had that day heard testimony from a Jew who had crawled out of a huge trench of earth. The victims had been brought by an Eichmann train to Poland. They were forced to dig the enormous ditch, then were shot. By the hundreds upon hundreds. Layers of earth were shoveled over layers of bodies.

The witness said softly: "I watched from the shadows. The earth heaved and rolled and finally stopped. I ran to the forest."

In the courtroom, a woman reporter for *Time* magazine, seated beside me, sobbed uncontrollably. How does a Jewish newsman console a reporter for *Time* magazine?

In the garden of the pension that night, Servatius' secretary also sobbed. "When I get back to Germany," she said, "I'll never believe what the older people will ever say to me again about what happened."

Adolf Eichmann.

Hundreds of newsmen were there to watch this pinch-faced, long-nosed super clerk for Hitler face his accusers. Mild mannered now. Exceedingly polite. Even when one witness told how he had been allowed to enter the presence of this man to plead that a large number of Jews be allowed to escape to Switzerland. Part of the ill-fated blood for trucks proposal.

The Jewish witness testified that the swastika-clad Eichmann required him to stand at attention at the far end of the room. Close, the Jew would have contaminated the German's air.

Eichmann's face flushed to hear this testimony. He tried to maintain a stoic expression. Seated at each side were two Jewish guards—all three breathing the same air inside a glass cage.

In my mind's eye I could conceive a new set of circumstances: Adolf Eichmann again wearing a Nazi uniform, commanding the gathering process of human cargo for waiting trains. Again, master of the logistics of death. One must deliver fuel to the ovens of Auschwitz, or Treblinka, or Sobibor, or Majdanek.

What a pity to allow the fires to go out!

Two months of this and I had enough. The documentation by this time was incomprehensible. Witnesses told how Jewish girls were tattooed across their breasts: "Feld Hur"—to be used by the Aryans until impregnated. Then transported to the ovens.

Macabre sadism of a sophisticated nation that had gone mad; this was told over and over again. There was no escaping it.

The railroad tracks of Europe must have a transcending tale to tell. I would one day travel them—to tell their story. All the way from Salonika to Vienna to Krakow to Warsaw. To the charnel houses of German furies!

I left Israel and flew to Switzerland.

I found a tiny hotel room in Zurich and collapsed on a bed. My beard was extended when I realized I'd not left that bed around the clock.

Hunger blended with sorrow and there was nothing I could do about it but sob.

Hymie, from Claremont Avenue, crying.

3

For years I nurtured that inner whim to take the tortured tracks to Auschwitz—to actually ride the rails, to scan the fields traversed by a people being relocated to eternity. Men, women, children; scholars, scientists, educators, carpenters (Jesus wasn't the only carpenter to come of our people and he was hardly the only Jew to die on a cross); young girls with embryos of genius within them; young boys who might have enriched a world with art and music and healing.

Morbid?

The great reality of the twentieth century was government's capacity to create death in a multitude of ways. But of all the ways, Zyklon B gas was to become a sublime national pastime as a sophisticated nation gave itself over to a macabre manufacturing process: Death.

Because I recognized the morbid magnetism of the whim that pulled me to the tracks that led to Auschwitz, the tracks of Adolf Eichmann, I found other diversions. Oh, I made it once to Moscow, three times to Poland, fourteen times to Israel—

always by air. Once, first class by train: Warsaw to Krakow. But the tracks of the Orient Express—from Istanbul to Salonika, then west and north to Vienna, the tracks of a people's sorrow—these I avoided.

A meeting with Elie Wiesel, during an interview at the Beverly Hilton Hotel, persuaded me that I ought to try. Otherwise, the German would have won another victory. This, I determined not to permit.

On another level: do I have the right to do this strange travel book when a creative generation of survivors of Holocaust is still here to tell the story? And of course, scanning the countryside of Europe through the windows of memory on a second-class train—would I not be the intruder?

Oh, screw it.

I was the kid called Abie Kabbible by the tough Polacks two blocks away. My father told me of the hatred for Jews that spread poison tentacles through the land of Paderewski. Church inspired? Was it not Church inspired, there, in Polonia where Jewish life flourished before the Church moved in a thousand years ago?

Two nations had lived there in Poland side by side for a thousand years—in near isolation, one from the other. Jews gave to Poland an elan of brilliance. Vilna, the Jerusalem of Poland, was the center of Talmudic studies, of brilliant scholarship. Warsaw's Jewish intelligentsia was foremost in the arts, the sciences, theater. Here in Warsaw was the flowering of Jewish journalism. And Lublin, Lublin—and its Academy of learning.

Hardly a Jew plowed the fields of Poland. Agrarian life was barred to the Jew. And so he flourished in the cities. Small flats became clothing factories by day, bedrooms by night. Trade, export and import, was developed for Poland by Jewish enterprise. There were important Jewish sports figures to emerge from Poland. And grand masters in chess.

Poland handed a world of laughter to a world that laughed

but hardly understood that a *shtetl* was a compound for Jews in which to live, such as they called peripheral living.

The toughest fighters for Poland in the war against the Nazis were the Jews. Indeed, in all Poland's wars! But that hardly mattered when it came to turning a Jew over to the German in exchange for a loaf of bread.

On one of my early trips to Warsaw, U.S. Ambassador John Cabot and I spoke about the remarkable fact that every significant death factory was located inside Poland.

"The German people themselves wouldn't stand for an Auschwitz in Germany," said Cabot. "There is such a thing as a national shudder. Germans would have shuddered had the death camps been located inside Germany. In Poland, that was another matter."

Culpability. Everything depends on whose rear is being gored by what ox.

Oh there were terror camps enough inside Germany: Dachau, Bergen-Belsen, Theresienstadt—but death was a by-product of those camps. They were holding camps, primarily. Auschwitz, Treblinka, Majdenek, Sobibor—these were slaughterhouses.

And the world knew—all the way back to Hitler's *Mein Kampf*—what was intended for the Jews. To the silence of the civilized world.

For a time, in Chicago, I had joined the Nazi party, attending meetings at the Haus Vaterland on Western Avenue across from Riverview Park. I was tall, blond, blue-eyed. I looked Aryan enough.

I alerted Jewish groups about planned marches of the German-American Bund in Harms Park near Skokie—swastika-clad hoodlums marching in America for *Deutschland Über Alles.* It was estimated that as many as five million Americans were part of the German-American Bund movement. The stunning hatred for Jews poured from their eyes and mouths. Germanic venom. It was hardly secret.

And during the Passover of 1943, American soldiers in Texas (I was one of them) were told by our officers that the Germans were embarking on a calculated program of extermination for the Jews of Europe. It was then that I learned of the Ghetto Uprising in Warsaw, and it seemed I followed the agonies of the time, moment by moment, but only in prayer.

Oh, to drop a hand grenade out of a Piper Cub over Berlin! Just a single hand grenade, or even a firecracker.

Franklin Roosevelt refused to order the bombing of Auschwitz (was it because I.G. Farben Industries had its huge synthetic rubber plant there?) and while armies ground themselves to bits, Adolf Eichmann was scrounging a continent for rolling stock to gather the Jews and Gypsies of Europe.

Why the Gypsies?

But then, why the Jews?

*   *   *

I asked Jacob Glatstein, the poet, whether a Jew who had not been directly part of the tragedy of the Holocaust may write about it. Glatstein said I may not.

Chaim Grade, another Yiddish poet, said that I may not be silent.

Elie Wiesel, who lived the German madness from within, told me I must go on.

And so, in early August of 1978, after a few days in Israel, simply to walk the fields and hills and shores of the Jewish state—I flew to Istanbul to seek my Orient Express and ride the iron rails to hell.

On the Orient Express

No crystal chandeliers, no svelte
Ladies beckon to the mysteries of me
Of why I'm here to touch the sadness
Of a glitter train's decay.

Exquisite glamor of intrigue
That once extended cigarettes
To circle smoke rings of diplomatic ruse
Through scheming smiles. Gone.

Glitter's given way to stink
Of dirty feet aboard a languid
Orient Express that snails Europa
On its thudding wheels that strike
In morose rhythms, these tracks

The water closet stinks
The whole train stinks
But, but there was drama
Murder enough
Once, on the Orient Express

AUGUST 18, 1978
EN ROUTE TO SALONIKA

5

As a child in Chicago, I was enchanted with spelling songs. Never could carry much of a tune. But darn if I couldn't spell "Harrigan" with the best of 'em. Listen, pick out the tune.

"Aitch-aye-double-are-eye-gee-aye-enn spells Harrigan."

Then came Con-stan-tinople—"C-o-n-s-t-a-n-t-i-n-o-p-l-e."

And when the world beyond my Claremont Avenue sang "Dardanella" my every fibre pleasured. I knew the words. Oh, I don't now. But it hardly matters, now.

What matters was that I found myself in Constantinople and its teeming Bosporus, the upper straits to the Black Sea. Took an excursion through the Bosporus almost to the Soviet waters—humming "Con-stan-tinople" all the way.

"Look, Ma; look, Pa—behind me are the Dardanelles. Me, Hymie!"

And to the north, beyond, far beyond, were the Russians whom my father served in 1905 during the Russian-Japanese War. And where my mother was born in Pietrokov, Minsky Gubernia.

I felt pretty much the sense of discovery that had grabbed

the poet Keats upon first looking into the page of "Chapman's Homer"—

> Then felt I like some watcher of the skies
> When a new planet swims into his ken
> Or like stout Cortez when with eagle eyes
> He stared at the Pacific, and all his men
> Looked at each other with a wild surmise
> Silent, upon a peak in Darien.

It wasn't "stout Cortez," it was "brave Balboa"—but who's counting?

But first, backtrack a bit.

I'd come to Jerusalem three weeks ago (at this writing). Couldn't sleep, so at three o'clock in the morning (ah, another song!) I was out walking the streets of the ancient city, the first of my kin to walk these streets of Jewish history in the treasured City of David.

Enthralled, communing with thoughts of Prophets and of eternity, I was suddenly brought smack to reality. A hooker had emerged from the shadows and had come up to me with an age-old suggestion. In that moment I knew the young Jewish nation had come of age.

Next day I heard them singing "Mack the Knife" in Hebrew. The holy language!

What am I saying? That while I may not divest myself of historic memory, survival itself requires that I grab history by the neck, look it in the eye, and when necessary exclaim: "Screw you!" to those who chart my demise. Beyond them, I can scan the beauties of a wild flower touched by an awakening day; I can sail the Dardanelles and wonder the fate of the gods of Greece and Rome, scanning treasured horizons. Indeed, what the hell ever happened to the gods of Greece and Rome?

Alas, mine is a legacy only of the survivors.

So many did not survive Babylon, nor Rome, nor the Crusades, nor the very Church of Rome in Spain, nor the pogroms, nor the German.

Ever hear of a gink called Bogdan Chmielnicki? Around 1648, Chmielnicki and his Cossacks cut a swath of death through the Jewish towns of Central Europe. A Polish army led by Czarniecki, supported by townspeople, also wreaked havoc on Jewish communities. Jews fought desperately against Chmielnicki at the fortress of Tulchin, where they were abandoned by the Poles.

Nine hundred thousand Jews died in the bloodbaths. Without a *mea culpa* from Rome.

* * *

I found soon enough that it's a lot easier entering Turkey by air than departing by train. The bureaucracy is startling, one finds, in trying to buy a railroad ticket from Istanbul. There is a queue to obtain proper credentials to join another queue to plunk down hard cash for other credentials in order to return to the first queue to show that payment had been made at the previous queue and for tickets now to be issued.

A mass of humanity surged toward the train; here, the end of the European line for the Paris to Constantinople run of the Orient Express.

There were no moments to consider the death of a myth; there were no white-gloved attendants on this Orient Express. Students rolled out their sleeping bags into the aisles, some bound for Sweden, others for Holland, Germany, Ireland. I found a seat in a depressing compartment. An obtuse sadness grabbed me.

This was the starting point of the train that carried madness in boxcars. On these tracks.

It would be 26 hours upon this train to Salonika, the city which once contained a flowering of Jewish life along the shores of the Mediterranean. In one breath it was denuded of Jewish life on orders of Adolf Eichmann: forty to sixty thousand were selected for transport west and north. An entire literature exists describing the event. But who in all the world is really aware of it? A lonely father who fled to the mountains to survive—and returned to disaster? A young mother turned prostitute to save the life of a child?

I find myself in a compartment with two Egyptians who had come on holiday to Istanbul and now by train to Athens—twelve hours beyond Salonika. I am wearing a leather belt with a "Jerusalem" buckle. I'd bought it at an Arab *shuk* in the Old City of Jerusalem, I tell the Egyptians. Their English is excellent. They smile.

Two swarthy men join the compartment. They speak Arabic. The Egyptian tells me they are from Iraq.

I cover my belt buckle. I've known for a long time that there is implacable hatred in Iraq for Jews. They are staunch suppor-ters of PLO terrorists. Would this be a nightmare ride—drama on the Orient Express? One of the Iraqis leaves to confer with another Arab in the passageway outside the compartment. I watch as the Iraqi (he has a surly expression) exchanges five $100 bills with the man. It may be paranoia, but I hear Arabic sounds that come through as "PLO" and "Arafat." It doesn't help to cover my belt buckle with folded arms. The word "Jerusalem" is also burnished into the leather in inch-high letters. Easily seen.

Suddenly the thought: should they attack—how to defend?

A Jewish editor who had been with the Israeli army at Kilometer 101 in Egypt and at Sassa, 16 miles from Damascus, would be a good enough catch.

"You still haven't written your article about the West Bank," I say to myself. "When will you write that story?"

"Shut up!" I shout inwardly. They might read my thoughts.

The swarthy Iraqi offers a small cake to the Egyptian and his wife. Arabs can now eat—it is *Ramadan,* the month when Moslems may not consume food during daylight hours.

Surprisingly, the Iraqi offers a cake to me. But I'd eaten, I explain, in gratitude. The surly Iraqi stirs awake, his surliness compounded by his discomfort. The Egyptian's wife starts to sneeze. She has a cold, the Egyptian explains. I offer some aspirins and they are grateful. Evening darkens and while the surly Iraqi is again asleep, his friend leaves, only to return moments later to announce that there is a car he'd found with a number of vacant compartments. Sleeping there would be more comfortable. The Egyptians leave with him for the other car. The surly Iraqi takes over the entire side of the compartment, kicks his shoes off to emit a foot stench, and soon is stretched out the length of the seat.

It seems that I detect the outline of a revolver under his arm. He looks up at me and says in surprising English: "I don't sleep three days from Iraq to Istanbul."

Seated in a corner of the bench, I scratch out what I perceive to be a lousy poem about the Orient Express — once the train of intrigue. Damn it, this train isn't headed for Shangri-La. And the tracks are blood red.

The other Iraqi comes into the compartment to sit down beside me, then suddenly announces that I may have the entire seat. He will find another place. Nice guy. Yet, I doze off with a troubled eye upon the surly one.

Suddenly, at 2 a.m., the train is halted on the border of Turkey and Greece. "Passports inspection!" Exit cards must be filled out. Turkey and Greece are not speaking these days — over their troubles in Cyprus.

The surly Iraqi can't fill out his exit card. He doesn't seem to know his name and age. I help him to read the birthdate on his passport: 1951. He fills out only a few of the spaces required by the Turkish border guards. When a guard stamps my card, and then stamps the Iraqi's, I detect a sigh of relief.

Now comes a swift contraband check by the Turkish police. They want to look inside the Iraqi's valise. Not mine. I am American, after all. I think I see what may be a red *kafiya,* the headcovering of a member of the PLO, in the Iraqi's valise. The

Turkish border guard O.K.'s the valise; we stretch out again—and a few minutes later we're in Greece. The train shudders as cars are being separated. Now another two hours of border checks, this time by Greek authorities. The Egyptian couple had now rejoined us—but not the second Iraqi.

The Egyptian's wife says the other Iraqi didn't come out of the compartment when the train was separated—he must by now be on his way to Bulgaria.

That's one Iraqi less! Suddenly a German-speaking man joins our compartment. He is tall and husky. Damn if I don't feel a sense of relief at his presence in the compartment. He is a student on his way to Frankfurt. More passport checks, the German evaporates, the Iraqi asks for my help with the Greek entry forms. Helping the Iraqi and feeling his gratitude, he no longer seemed threatening. Perhaps I was wrong about the gun outline under his arm. The train, which is painfully slow, halts at a Greek village. Morning lights appear in the sky. Conversation crosses in all directions in the compartment.

The Egyptian couple is on holiday from their home in Ismailia. I had been across the Suez Canal from Ismailia a number of times during the Israeli occupation. My traveling companions were among the fortunate ones—their home had been spared by the war. No, he didn't have to serve in Sadat's army during the Yom Kippur War. His work as an agronomist was very important to the state. His wife also had an agriculture degree. No, he hadn't met the Iraqi before we boarded the train in Istanbul. "He always sleeps," said the Egyptian woman. The Iraqi wakes at this point to offer me a cigarette. I tell him I do not smoke. Perhaps he'd like a peach. I'd come aboard with bread, cheese, mineral water and peaches. Peaches were in exquisite season now.

The train moves painfully throught the morning country- side. It is hard to transfer feelings. We pass rust-colored box cars on sidings. They were old enough to have been pressed into service by Eichmann. Each has an air hatch high up in the car. I presume a tall man might be able to peer out of the small opening to scan the skies. Or to scream for help.

The train grinds to a halt at the station of another village. The Iraqi gets out of the compartment—and we see him streaking across the tracks toward a small group of buildings. Out of view. Was all of it, the *kafiya,* the outline of a gun, the hundred dollar bills, the mention of Arafat and the PLO just part of another nightmare?

Suddenly, from the cluster of buildings, the Iraqi again comes into view. He is rushing back to the train, cradling a watermelon in his arms.

A vendor appears near the train and a number of pas-sengers rush out to buy sacks of fruit. I buy a sack of peaches for my beautiful friends in the compartment.

The Iraqi slices his watermelon with a huge pocket knife. Ramadan is forgotten. We exchange watermelon for peaches. Fears had long since melted. The fruit is heady, of humanity; the quality of kindness and wine.

"I am a Kurd. Do you know of the Kurds?" asks the Iraqi.

My heart goes out to him. He is leaving Iraq to take a job of some sort in Germany. Do I know of the Kurds? An entire nation of Kurds was being systematically eliminated in a mur-derous genocide by the Iraq government; caught in a vise without possible escape to Iran.

Clearly, in the sunlight, there is no gun under his right armpit. Nighttime apprehensions bring on their own distor-tions. The train starts rolling again. I tell the Iraqi (the Egyptians listen intently) that on these railroad tracks the Germans had collected the Jewish people for relocation. To Auschwitz. He knows and his eyes glisten. How many tragedies had he beheld in the destruction of his people?

"I hope there will be peace," I say to my friends as the train finally rolls into Salonika.

The Iraqi and the Egyptian help me with my bags. The Iraqi insists on handing them down to the Egyptian through the compartment window. The Egyptian had rushed off the train just to be helpful.

I clasp his hand and we embrace.

I reach up to the Iraqi and for the first time in my life exchange a Roman armclasp with another.

May we all go with God!

I was numb on arrival in Salonika.

The city is now called Thessaloniki. But since this is a personal journey, it hardly matters by what name the city is called. Through the years of Jewish imprint upon this city—when the Sabbath for everyone was on Saturday—it was called Salonika.

Coming to this ancient city required 26 hours aboard a disoriented Orient Express, second-class all the way! I took a room at the Capsis Hotel adjoining the new Thessaloniki railroad station and konked out.

The Jewish community of Thessaloniki offers this bit of historical data from its archives, a small pamphlet given to visitors:

"Since the foundation of Thessaloniki in the 4th century before the Common Era, Jews could surely be found among the first inhabitants.

"Towards the middle of the first century, when Apostle Paul visited the city, he found a powerful and prosperous Jewish

population. Soon after the Middle Ages, she received the fugi-
tives of Central Europe and many runaways coming from Italy;
and when the Inquisition started its sinister task in the Iberian
peninsula, Spanish and Portugese Jews came in massive
waves—especially in 1492, 1537 and 1650.

"Also, many Jews of Central Europe arrived in large crowds
between 1648 and 1659, when the Cossacks annihilated three
hundred Jewish communities.

"In the 16th century, the Jews strengthened their prepon-
derance in Thessaloniki, which became the homestead and
crucial point of Judaism.

"Trade took an impressive development. The port was in
direct contact with all the European ports. Thessaloniki became an industrial, commercial and financial center of the first
order.

"But it was the scientific, literary and religious fields that
set her up as a real metropolis of Israel. Colleges and illustrious
seminaries perpetuated the traditions of high culture. Students
from all corners (of the world) were coming with the purpose of
consulting the rich collection of books gathered by the Benve-
niste, Perahia and many other families. The books published by
her writers covered all the fields of human knowledge at the
time."

*   *   *

I had known that Salonika was one of a handful of cities in
the world that offered a haven for Jews fleeing the Catholic
Holocaust in Spain and Portugal. Jewish scholars refer to the
tragedy in a delicate term—"Inquisition"—without pointing the
crime directly at a still unrepentant Church.

By whose authority may they or anyone inquire of my faith?

The humiliation of forced conversion to a Trinity that would
use the cross as a sword and love as an inflamed stake.

Bitter thoughts surge through me as I head for the central

Jewish community headquarters in Salonika, in the morning.

Was there an Adolf Eichmann in Iberia in 1492?

Oh, indeed there was: Torquemada, the converted Jew who ravaged his people to prove his new, greater faith. However Jews might flee, they fled the furies of a clergy gone mad. And out of a population in Iberia estimated as high as 700,000 Jews, when the Catholic flame began simmering, only 70,000 of our people survived as Jews.

Only a fragment of these came to Salonika. Others went north to Holland; some to the West Indies where on the island of St. Eustatius, Jewish "Marranos" (the Spanish word for pigs, because they had reverted to Judaism) became the gun runners for the armies of George Washington until captured by the British and sent off in exile to St. Thomas Island. Another forgotten exodus.

The 70,000 surviving Iberian Jews left the land, carrying out with them a Golden Age of beauty, literature, song. Indeed, in Spain they still sing the Jewish songs of that Golden Age, assuming that the poets were Spaniards. But then, the German sang to his "Lorelei" in his frozen tank at Stalingrad. Author unknown.

Thus, the Judeo-Spanish language of Ladino came to Salonika just as the Yiddish of Central Europe came, for a generation or two, to America—even to win for America a Nobel Prize in literature through Isaac Bashevis Singer.

A microcosm of the tragedy of Salonika is indicated by events which overwhelmed the Greek island of Rhodes. Dr. Marc D. Angel, in his work, *The Jews of Rhodes,* traces the history of Jewish life on that fascinating island to 1523 when Jews expelled from Spain started to arrive. Out of a Rhodes Jewish population that at one time totalled 4,000, only six Jews remain on the island. More than a thousand were taken aboard the Eichmann express, called Orient.

*   *   *

I am aware that in a travel book statistics may become unnerving. Yet, to set the background, this must now be told. It is reported briefly in the historical data given to me by Salomon H. Perahia, the Salonika Jewish community's very learned director.

"At the start of the 20th century, the Jews of Thessaloniki numbered 90,000, constituting more than half of the city's population. In 1908, due to the exodus of the laboring classes to the United States of America, a downward tendency became evident.

"The great fire of 1917 left 50,000 Jews homeless, as a result of which a large emigration wave followed to the Western countries. The major portion settled in Paris, thus increasing considerably the colony of Thessaloniki Jews established there."

An anti-Jewish wave swept the city in 1932, provoked by the Hitler-like EEE (anti-Semitic nationalist association) and some 14,000 Jews fled to Palestine. Thus, at the time of the 1940 census, the Jews of Salonika numbered 49,000.

It took only a few weeks of German occupation to destroy the centuries-old Jewish community of Salonika.

Out of 46,091 Jews deported to Auschwitz and other death camps, only 1,950 managed to return—thus only 4 per cent survived. A city in Jewish history had lost 96 per cent of its population to German gas and cremation.

Mr. Perahia told me:

"The hell victims arrived in small groups, gradually. They came as rotten pieces of nature, excoriated human beings. They expected to be welcomed with bands and flowers. Cruel disappointment: there was nothing here in the city to receive them. Not the least organized help. The Joint Distribution Committee appeared on the scene a year later."

German indemnification of the victims was really a joke, says Perahia. "The people were dead. Who would ask indemnification for them?"

During four centuries, Salonika "was a real Jewish city," he said. "The arrivals from Iberic countries had imposed their language and customs. The entire city did not work on Saturdays and the Great Holidays of the Jewish calendar."

In time, the Jewish color faded. Sunday became the day of rest, although Jewish merchants closed their shops two days rather than infringe the Sabbath commandment.

How did the Germans put into effect the destruction of the Jewish community of Salonika?

"They set up a special ghetto near the old train station because a large Jewish quarter was there," Perahia said. "When you leave the new station, a kilometer in front of you was the old station. They took everyone: the intellectuals, the crippled, the sick, the old and the young.

"I lost my mother. I lost one brother and his son; one brother and his wife and a little girl. My wife's mother was lost, her father and her sister. If you have in mind that we lost 96 per cent of our population killed—there was no people who lost that much."

How did he survive?

Mr. Perahia, now 79, said he fled to Athens and hid with Christian friends. Athens was under the control of Italy at the time. Upon the fall of Italy, he witnessed the intrusion of German forces into the historic Greek capital city.

They destroyed the old Jewish cemetery in Salonika.

"Nothing was left. They wanted to erase our memories."

Salonika's new university is now built upon those memories.

"It was a very large cemetery," he said. "From 1560 to 1940 is a long time."

Only a thousand Jews are left today in their Thessaloniki. The survivors are rebuilding their institutions, schools and ties to Israel and world Jewry. There is great joy at the community center upon the annual independence day anniversary of Israel—and the Day of Mourning for victims of the Holocaust touches all.

Once there was a large daily Ladino newspaper published

for Jews of Salonika, plus two daily French language Jewish newspapers, several weeklies and book publishing houses.

Today, only one Greek language newspaper comes out twice a month for the surviving Jews of the city. Additionally, at least half a dozen books have appeared in recent years, including an illustrated Haggadah for Passover, published in 1970 in three languages: Ladino, Greek and Hebrew.

I leave the community building. The men in the card room are anxious for Mr. Perahia to return.

I walk toward the seacoast and notice a movie house that is offering a stirring bill: "The Death Machines." Subtitled: "The Killers of the Future are Ready Now" —starring Ron Marchini, Michael Chong and Joshua Johnson.

Along the Aegean Sea, the beer is excellent. I stroll on a lovely Sunday noon toward the city's landmark, the Salonika Tower. It is a large circular building, constructed of rock. A former prison.

A nearby ferryboat crew calls out to me—a ride to the beach, only 50 minutes away.

The sea air cleanses my thoughts as the beautiful, old city moves away in the sunshine.

Now, this being a travel book, I might suggest the Salonika beach across a charming bay offers an idyllic setting.

But being the kind of travel book this is, I must admit that I remained aboard the ferry for the return to Salonika. Many thoughts bombarded me as the boat was being cradled by soft Aegean waves.

Jonah rode these waves.

Other memories ago.

One must become steel for the section of track leading from Salonika, across Yugoslavia and on into Austria, to Vienna, the city of "Anschluss" where German troops were embraced by the Austrians and Hitler knew that now Europe was his. Hitler, after all, was Austrian. The Viennese waltzes played no love songs for the Jewish people.

I board the train in Salonika before dawn. The previous day, being Sunday, did not permit the purchase of food for another 25 hours aboard train. I found a small shop open in Salonika that offered sweet cakes for sale. For a sweet ride.

The Orient Express twisted and struggled through sullen, barren Serbian fields to the city of Nis; then past miles and miles of cornfields, protected occasionally by small brick fortresses with holes for machine guns or rifles.

I see no Gypsies in Yugoslavia. The Croatian puppet regime of Ante Pavlik, which served Hitler during World War II, had delivered them to death—treated as subhumans, just as were Jews. Seventy thousand Jews once lived in these cities and villages. All massacred by the Ustashi, the murder arm of the Croatians. I see no signs of past Jewish life as the train weaves a pathway of bitterness across Yugoslavia.

In my mind's eye I recall a three-week immigration hearing I covered in Los Angeles, in 1958. Yugoslavia had requested the United States to return a key minister of the Croatian regime to stand trial in Belgrade for his role in the mass murder of hundreds of thousands of Serbs, Jews and Gypsies. The immigration officer took hours of testimony from witnesses to the crimes. The charges were directed against Andrija Artukovic, mastermind of the Croatian killers.

A number of Catholic priests took the witness stand to testify that Artukovic was "a fine family man." One priest admitted that he had himself fired a gun during the days of Croatian power. Just pointed the rifle out of a door and fired, he said.

The immigration officer ruled that Artukovic's crime was a political one and he was allowed to remain at his home in Surfside, California. Asylum in America.

Each day during the hearing, Artukovic was surrounded by a half-dozen henchmen—the Ustasha in America.

Once, during the hearings, I shot Artukovic: a flash bulb in his face.

"Which newspaper are you from?" he asked.

"The Jewish newspaper," I answered.

Lines on his face tightened. His jowls drained of color.

Because there were four or five priests in constant attendance at the hearing, I had arranged for a young, handsome, bearded rabbi to join me at the press table. Two can play the game!

Simon Wiesenthal, the Nazi hunter, later told me during a California interview that Artukovic is one of the most bloodthirsty men breathing the American air of freedom.

But Yugoslavia has a Communist regime and sending Artukovic back was not part of the American game plan. Not then, at least. In July, 1981, the U.S. immigration authorities ordered Artukovic deported. But an appeal to the courts was promptly filed, and at 81 years Artukovic was still residing in protective sanctuary in America.

*   *   *

Over rivers of great beauty in Yugoslavia goes our train; through long tunnels cut into steep mountains. We are now surrounded by huge pine forests, from which the partisans fought to stall advances of the German.

The fields are being worked by women. There are no tractors in sight. Through the small villages, in a day of missiles to the stars, carts are being drawn by oxen.

Quaint sights for dowagers peering out at the countryside from an elegant Orient Express. For them, as for us, the train ride from Istanbul to Paris may have been lengthy and tiresome—more tiresome for those of us riding the latter day Orient, now that air travel had stripped the elegance and crystal from this post World War I vintage train.

We are now being transported in cars of filth: drafty, noisy, the wheels gnashing against separations between rails, producing eerie rhythmic patterns, the sound of fingernails scratching school blackboards.

If the ride was tiresome and exceeding slow on this strange train, the time passed all too swiftly for the Jews (mostly Jews, almost always Jews!) packed into wooden box cars for the inelegant ride to Auschwitz, standing all the way, or expiring on the spot. Men and women clawed their box cars in vain attempts to break out. In Poland, peasants sold snowballs to the victims—for diamonds. How to eliminate human waste aboard this incredible Eichmann form of transport? It all happened 35 years ago.

*   *   *

The train is packed with students from all parts of Europe. They had boarded the previous evening in Athens. Backpacks were rolled out on every stretch of aisle space.

To be assured compartment space, I had paid a special fee to the ticket agent. Unfortunately, I had displaced two German girl students who had no tickets. One exclaimed: "Oh *sheiss!*" as I flopped into the tight compartment seat. I had managed to buy a liter of mineral water at the station in Salonika. That and the two cakes would have to suffice for food. I had no Yugoslavian money to buy anything.

Our train is now through the mountains and again into fields of corn. Miles of corn. I see no tractors. Suddenly, another mass of freight cars and we approach Belgrade. We now have a "restaurant" car attached to our Orient Express. It is dingy, offering crude salami sandwiches and black beer. The attendant will give me 13 bottles of Yugoslavian beer for an American $10 note. I notice he has cartons of cheese available for sandwiches. A small carton of cheese and two beers for $10. Great. A Communist ripoff, but that's the way it is. I suddenly remember I'd brought along some halvah from Israel and there were some dried apricots left in one of my sacks. A feast! I share the bounty with two medical students from Ireland who hadn't eaten in two days.

We were grabbed back to reality by this passion for food and human needs. But it is different now from the days of rolling box cars. There is no gun at my back.

It may be a Communist country, but "tourists" are being fleeced as in Paris or London or Istanbul.

A sharpie goes through the train offering a gold bracelet for 400 dinar. Gold? In a pig's ear. The train proceeds slowly through Belgrade, past large apartment complexes which are direct copies of those I'd seen in Moscow seventeen years earlier. I notice there are now many automobiles on the roads and a freeway system appears in operation. But oxen still pull wagons through the streets. They roll on pneumatic tires.

Then, corn again, for miles on end. I imagine "Injun Summer" in the Middle West and recall the famous McCutcheon cartoon in the Chicago *Tribune*. Why? I hardly know.

Two tall girls from Germany find seats in the compartment. They are wearing short shorts. Goosepimples cover their thighs in the chilly compartment. They are on their way to Vienna and then by car to Bucharest. Stretched out in her bedroll in the aisle nearby is a young girl, a medical student from Denmark, reading Irwin Shaw's *Rich Man, Poor Man*.

Suddenly the train halts adjoining a corn field. Waiting, I suppose, as the box cars would wait for a passing train. *(Did a suggestion of hope stir victims as their train halted—or did they want to get on with it?)* The sun is descending swiftly. It is 7:20 p.m., Belgrade time.

Midnight we are in Zagreb where we lose most of our students. They are now in a separated section of the train, heading for Germany. The train is being swept for the first time. Bottles, debris are everywhere. Water closets are dreadful. Toilet paper is nonexistent. Urine covers the floors.

We go through customs again. Each border crossing has its own moments of drama. Passports are inspected. Tickets are examined. The train crosses into Austria and the process is repeated.

By this time I am inured to the lack of sleep. At 4 a.m. I am able to discern the Austrian countryside: lush, green hills, beautiful homes in the hills and valleys through which the tracks lead. Farms stretch blankets of growth over hills and the farm homes are exquisite in Alpine beauty. (The very same farmers were here, for the most part, when Hitler was greeted with cheers of welcome. They were part of the storm of voices that filled the radio airwaves from Europe.)

The train is due to arrive in Vienna by 8 a.m.—August 22, a Tuesday morning. I must quickly find a hotel because I have no plans to spend much time in this city beside its melancholy Danube.

After a shower and a few hours of rest, I have plans to visit Simon Wiesenthal at his incredible Documentation Center in Vienna.

But for the moment, as the train approaches the city of Anschluss, I hear no Viennese waltzes. (Oh, they were played for Jews who were selected for extermination at Birkenau—the hellhole section of Aushchwitz.)

A Gypsy-dressed woman joins my compartment, clad in black dress, black scarf, black jacket. A fat German woman is seated to my right. She is curious to know what I am writing in my notebook.

She was old enough to have shouted with the loudest of them when Hitler came to Austria.

As we approach the railroad station, I notice a large bill-board sign declaring: *"Arbeit—Freiheit—Sicherheit."*

"Work—Freedom—Security."

But then— *"Arbeit Macht Frei!"*

Slogans *über alles.*

8

I had been on a mission to Vienna 12 years ago. Came in by train from Switzerland to pick up some stories for *Heritage*. But immediately upon arrival, I was put to bed with very high fever. I had a suite at the new Intercontinental Hotel. (I vomited in the shrubs in front of the hotel, which convinced me that perhaps a report on Vienna had better be postponed.) Two days of medication and I had taken the first plane out to Budapest, to await a flight to Warsaw.

From the air, I scanned the Danube. If brown is blue, then I'm a Shinto priest. That's all I saw of Vienna, the once glitter city. The beautiful blue Danube. A river of excrement.

This time, a call to the office of Simon Wiesenthal came up with the information that the Nazi hunter was out of town but would be back the next morning. Perhaps he would see me then. Which means a change in plans. Extending my Viennese "holiday" by a day, at least.

At the railroad station, I purchased a second-class ticket on the "Chopin Express" (as it is called) from Vienna to Krakow.

Auschwitz is situated at Oswiecim, about 30 miles west of Krakow.

"Do you want round trip tickets?" the sales agent asked.

I stared at him wryly.

"Jewish people never had the choice of round trip tickets to Krakow. Not when they had to leave Vienna 35 years ago."

He understood. Tried to smile, then frowned.

I called the Jewish Agency to try to meet with an information officer to pick up a story on how the process of Jewish migration from the Soviet Union to Vienna was going.

A woman who said her name was Malka told me that "The Boss" was not available and he was the only one who could arrange an interview.

"The Boss? What's his name?" I asked.

"He's just The Boss. Call me later and we'll see about the interview."

Well, indeed—as a protective measure, one does not give out names in Vienna, even to a caller who identifies himself as a Jewish editor from Los Angeles.

So I went by tram to the Jewish Community Building to collect some background about Jewish life in general, in Vienna.

I found a very large three-story building guarded by armed special police. My Los Angeles police press card served in good stead now, and I was allowed to enter. Indeed, within minutes I was meeting, through an interpreter, with Karl Lazer, director general of the community.

Before German Anschluss there were an estimated 220,000 Jews in Vienna. Lazer said that today there are 8,000 Jews in the city and its environs. What happened to the 212,000? Lazer, who himself had survived a number of German camps, shrugged.

Does he see a future for Jewish life in Vienna—a city which once was celebrated for its Jewish creativity?

"Of course," he responds. But I detect he isn't quite as certain as his words.

Can he compare Jewish life in Vienna with that of West Berlin?

"Jews of Berlin get help from the German government," he said. "Here, we get nothing from the government."

Austria admits to no culpability in the matter of the Holocaust. But there is a Jew who serves as Chancellor of Austria. (I make no attempt to meet with Bruno Kreisky, Austria's Jewish chancellor. Self-hatred is hardly a new fact in Jewish history. For reasons of state, Kreisky is more at home with Yassir Arafat than with his brother who lives in Israel.)

Interview with Lazer over (for I am not interested in details how Vienna Jews provide geriatric service to those who live there), I hasten to the center's entrance with my translator.

I ask him: "Are Jews of Vienna no longer afraid?"

"Afraid of what?" he responds. The old question in answer to a question.

I nod to the police guard who opens the door for me to depart.

"Oh, this is just in case," says the translator.

I leave the building.

*   *   *

I check the office of the Associated Press to attempt to learn the location of the Halfway House which processes Jewish arrivals from the Soviet Union. All the AP knows is that it is located somewhere in District 11 of Vienna. Not much help.

I keep calling the Jewish Agency and am told The Boss is not in. Try later. Later.

I take a tram to the Intercontinental Hotel. It no longer wears the elegant crystal chandelier feel of my earlier visit. I dine in the hotel's coffee shop, then cross to the lovely park nearby, where a concert of Strauss music is being played. Jewish prisoners—all first-rate musicians—were "selected" by the German to play this music for new arrivals at Auschwitz. Always Viennese waltzes—or so it seemed.

I leave for the center of town. Meeting with The Boss is by now out of question. At least for today. And Malka's voice on the telephone has taken on the aspect of annoyance.

"Hey, there's a McDonald's!" I almost shout.

Thoughts of an American-type of chocolate shake felt great suddenly. Heck with the diet. Look. At this McDonald's, seats are at a premium and every table is shared. Opposite are two students from the United States. They'd just left Israel where they had worked on archaelogical digs during the summer. Marvelous feeling to come upon countrymen at McDonald's, in Vienna.

At the table behind me are two women and a child. They are speaking in low voice. Suddenly the boy exclaims: *"Lama lo?"* "Why not?" in Hebrew.

I turn around with a warm: *"Shalom, shalom!"*

All the world is Jewish.

But then, so is exhaustion. I hasten to the Kongress Hotel, a flea bag, and collapse in bed.

This section of my travels must be told precisely. I have it all on tape. Nearly an hour of analysis of history as viewed through the eyes and mind of a Nazi hunter.

One phone call to the secretary of Simon Wiesenthal and I am told I might have fifteen or twenty minutes. If I'd come over at once.

Minutes later I enter the vestibule of what appears to be a converted apartment house, now an office building. Up the stairs to a door with a simple marker: "Documentation Center." The door swings open.

I notice the door could protect adequately against a sling shot fired at long range. There is a small office to the right where a secretary works. A young man leads me to the private library office of Simon Wiesenthal. The Nazi hunter is in shirtsleeves, answering a telephone call from Denmark.

One wall consists of a map of Europe showing the German centers of terror and destruction in Germany, Poland, Czechoslovakia under the Hitler "thousand-year reich." Another wall contains citations and awards to Wiesenthal, who played a key role in hunting down Adolf Eichmann. It is hardly necessary for me to spend time searching out his background and his rea- sons for hunting down the German madmen. Not during my fifteen or twenty minutes. Not on my time.

Get to the meat of it, Herb. Wiesenthal gets the point quickly. He says:

"I am here the people's number one enemy in Austria. Why?

"Because I find out, because I made a memo to the Austrian government ten years ago: the Austrians were only 8½ percent of the population of greater Germany, but the Austrians are responsible for fifty percent of the crimes."

How to trigger Wiesenthal to talk? Oh, I must come away with more than mere niceties and thank you. I tell him of my recent travels to Spain, that I had completed a book of poems on Spain, mostly about the role of the Catholic Church in the years of the Spanish Holocaust.

Wiesenthal springs up from his desk, his face flushed. I had triggered him:

"Hitler invented nothing! It took me twenty years time to realize the comparison. I had been looking for the sources of what had gone on in Germany—and so I am going back generations. Now I find evidence of all the knowledge of all the anti-Jewish laws that helped the Germans.

"If the Inquisition had the same technology as that of the time of Hitler, we would have had at that time the same prob- lems. Through the studies of the Spanish years I found out the very great guilt of the Catholic Church, because all this hatred by all churches, but especially the Catholic Church—they cost us millions of people. Not only Hitler!"

He was stalking his library, deep in thought. A powerful man, heavy set—he'd have to be powerful to singlehandedly create his documentation center to bring to justice the supreme madmen of history.

Wiesenthal is troubled by logistics.

"From the time of the Roman Empire, there were four million Jews: a half million in old Israel and three and a half million in all of the Roman Empire. At the same time the British Islands had a population of one million.

"The British developed from one million to more than fifty million. We developed from four million to fourteen million. If we had developed on the same levels as the British there would today be 200 million Jews because we were four times more populous.

"You see, on this simple example you can see not only what we lost in the Hitler period, but during all the history. Not only extermination was the problem, but forced assimilation. Even today in Spain a minimum of one to two million Spanish people are of Jewish origin."

Why has there been no Catholic *mea culpa*? I asked.

"I will tell you. Even the Communist regimes rehabilitated their victims. But the Catholic Church never, never made a trial again—a new trial: because they know from all their documents that so many people were tried on false testimonies. Not only Jews, but others.

"Years ago I made the proposal to the Church to make one trial, not against the Jew, but to clear the air . . ."

"Cervantes?" I suggested.

Wiesenthal laughed. "Cervantes was condemned to death because he said the world was round," he stated rather blandly. No, it would have to be on another level.

"I suggested that some man be placed on trial, and through this trial to rehabilitate this man and thus rehabilitate the Jewish people. But the Church don't accept it. They don't accept it."

The suggestion, said Wiesenthal, was made to high officials of the Church in the days of Pope John.

"This was a man who died too early," he said, sadly.

What of the declaration of the Ecumenical Council that has been so much celebrated?

"This was a compromise. It changed very little. It seems the

Church needs centuries to make changes." Then he was triggered by a problem of his own:

"I asked Cardinal Beer what was the consequence of the Church that all who put our people into concentration camps — they were young, they were from schools where they had courses in religion. What remained in them when the people of their religion can do this?"

Why were the death camps placed in Poland?

"At the Wannsee Conference when the Final Solution was spelled out by Heydrich, he knew that the local (Polish) population would not fight for the Jews. Local anti-Semites helped the Nazis because a part of the population profited by the Jewish tragedy. But a number of Poles did pay with their lives for helping Jews."

I quoted a statistic that I'd recently come upon—that only one percent of the Polish people gave some protection to the Jews of Poland. This was the lowest percentage of any people in Europe.

"If people knew that to give a Jew a piece of bread meant the death sentence, I don't know how many people in the United States would help," said Wiesenthal.

(He moved swiftly, too swiftly to another thought. It was in Poland, to a Catholic priest that I would shortly suggest that I didn't seek bravery in anyone. I did insist that no people on earth had the right to betray a Jew to the German for a loaf of bread. But that, dear reader, is later.)

Wiesenthal wanted to make a remarkable point here:

"The Polish gangsters (every country has gangsters)—they helped the Jewish gangsters. The Jewish thieves and the prostitutes and all were saved by their Polish colleagues. Why? Because they fought all their lives against the police. They knew all the steps and these Jews were from the same professions.

"From the other side, you had in Poland, except Yugoslavia, the biggest resistance against the Germans. This is not known in the world because the Communists falsified the history of the resistance.

"The Communist resistance against the Germans began after the war the Nazis started against Russia. In June of 1944, there was no Communist resistance in Poland against the Nazis. Not only this, but there was a collaboration between the Soviets and the Nazis against the Polish resistance.

"I found documentation about this. In the Soviet-occupied territories [he was at his wall map, waving his arms to show large sections] the Soviets used Jewish Communists against Polish patriots. The same was in Latvia. The same was in Lithuania. The same was in Estonia. The same was in all other places.

"The deportation of Latvian, Lithuanian and Estonian patriots was done by Jewish Communists. They handed them over. Yes, our people are also guilty.

"It is very easy to say that only one percent of the Poles helped the Jews. Look, these Jewish Communists, they took over top positions. The Polish Communist Party in Poland gave leading positions to the Poles. But the Executive was in the hands of the Jews.

"Half of Poland, in the division of the country with Hitler, came to the Russians. These people, these Jews, had immediately positions of power. A part of them are now in the United States and are anti-Communists. But after 1968, when Poland expelled its Jewish Communists and they came here to my office—I expelled them. Huh, I told them, 'Up to this moment, to this very moment you helped to persecute the others and now you are also persecuted and you say you are Jewish.' But at the time they were in power, they persecuted the Jews also. My father-in-law died as a Soviet prisoner arrested by Jewish Communists."

The fifteen or twenty minutes that had been allocated to me had long since passed. This travel journal suddenly was in on an

incredible analysis of Central European sadism. Savagery without parallel in history.

"All of this is known," Wiesenthal exclaimed. "And after the
war, all these people in the leading positions in Hungary and
Czechoslovakia, they arrested their political enemies. Who was
Slansky? A Jew, Saltzman. Who were the others? It was a
miracle that in 1956 we did not have an anti-Jewish problem in
Hungary. And in Romania—who was the whole Central Committee of the Communist Party? Anna Pauker was the boss.
Don't forget the Poles, they knew the role of the Jewish Communists against the Polish patriots."

"There are two factors: the Polish people had a deep hatred
against the Jewish people and also feared the Polish Jewish
Communists," I suggested.

"Yes."

"What about the educated Poles? Why were they silent?"

"The majority of the educated Poles were in the Polish
resistance. In the Polish resistance were also a number of Jews.
They helped the resistance. There were half a million people in
the resistance. They had more than a hundred radio stations. it
was a state within a state.

"The Poles were interested in waging war against the Nazis,
but they took direction from London which told them to wait
until the Soviets reach the Polish borders.

"Because of this, they could not help the Jewish rebellion in
1943 because they were preparing for the rebellion in 1944.
Through this, their help to the Jews could not be large. They
gave the Jews only a little."

The heartbreak logic of this I could not accept, even from a
Simon Wiesenthal.

Jews were being manufactured to death and Jewish fighters
in the ghettoes were left by the Polish resistance to fight alone. A
criminal decision in history, I noted.

Wiesenthal then exclaimed:

"We are making a huge mistake looking at everything from

the Jewish point of view. We are not the *pipik* of the world. You know what is the *pipik?* That is the mistake that all the other nations made."

My own *pipik,* my own bellybutton, tightened.

"There will come a time when the Jews will say, ah, the time of Henry Kissinger was a very good time."

I told him that after visiting Auschwitz and Warsaw, I planned a trip to Konin, the town west of Lodz where my father and the grandfather of Barry Goldwater were born.

"You will find nothing in Konin. I am sure they destroyed the Jewish cemetery. Everything."

Shall Jews turn their backs upon former Jewish shrines and historical sites?

"We survived because the history of man is the history of migration. For thousands of years people have come to one place from another. Jews are the exception because we don't mix. And this is one of the reasons for anti-Semitism."

"We are in Vienna," I said. "This is the city of *Anschluss.* Here all about you are the same people who cried out for Hitler. I see them in the streets and in the villages we went through."

"Yes, these are the same people," he said.

What was left to talk about?

10

But I must make one massive effort to meet The Boss!

I call the Jewish Agency from Wiesenthal's office. The Boss is busy. I will come to the Jewish Agency headquarters and will wait until he, or I, *plotz,* I tell Malka.

Wiesenthal's secretary gives me the address of The Boss and I leave the Documentation Center. Simon Wiesenthal walks me to the door and suddenly I cling fast to my tape recorder. What if it didn't work? A sinking thought!

I would see the Nazi hunter in California in November when he would come to attend the inauguration of the Wiesenthal Holocaust Center at Yeshiva University of Los Angeles.

Wiesenthal's young male assistant walks out with me. He says he is only a part-time employee. Funds are difficult to come by, and he helps out as needed.

The aide tells me that only a block away, on the square at the site of the Hotel Metropole, is a monument that merits attention.

This was Gestapo headquarters for Austria. The marker

stands across the road from where the headquarters was actually located. Near the stone marker is a tall statue of Lessing,
author of *Nathan the Wise,* a classic drama in the cause of
humanity. Its famous closing line comes back to me: "That
which makes me a Moslem in your eyes makes you a Jew in
mine."

The office of The Boss is only a few blocks away. A short
walk.

At the office door a voice calls out over a loudspeaker: "You
cannot enter because of security. You must call first for an
appointment."

Talk to the door and tell the door that you'd called innumer-
able times. Three times yesterday, many times today. Tonight I
leave for Krakow!

It hardly mattered. By this time, Malka was furious at my
insistence to see The Boss—and by this time I was curious to
see what The Boss looked like. To no avail.

I make it back to the park across from the Intercontinental
Hotel (I quickly learn the tram and bus systems of the various
cities). There is another Strauss concert being played under a
hot sun.

I am seated in a fragment of shade when a young man walks
past with his parents. He's wearing a DePaul University T-shirt. I
call out: "I went to DePaul once!"

(At the age of seventeen, during the Depression, I was
admitted to the DePaul Law School in Chicago. Because of the
Depression, I left the study of law two years later. A long lost
remembrance.)

The family tells me of their travel plans through Germany.
Then they ask where I'm heading.

"To light a candle at Auschwitz," I say.

Cold silence.

"It all began here and in Germany," I say. "It began with
Anschluss."

They walk away. The father remembers. I see it deep in his

eyes. He remembers something. But then, everyone here remembers.

Something.

*   *   *

I have a simple spaghetti dinner at a small sidewalk cafe. It's a Viennese restaurant that charges $5.50 for a single drink of Jim Beam. Coffee here is $1.26 per cup. No refills. Who won the war, indeed!

A bearded *Chassid* passes, with his wife and two children wearing *yarmulkes*. I want very much to reach out to them, but they seem in a hurry. In an earlier Viennese day, the *Chassid's* beard would have been pulled from his face. He is nattily dressed in black. The family speaks Hebrew.

Here, the *Chassid* is not afraid to walk the streets of romantic Vienna beside the Danube. But I've covered that. Also, that the Jewish center is on constant police patrol in a day that a Jewish chancellor is head of state in Austria.

And that, too, I covered.

So back to my flea bag hotel to pick up my luggage and to organize my new travels—aboard the Chopin Express to Krakow. This is a travel book, remember?

11

Simon Wiesenthal estimated that it took 11 or 12 days to transfer human cargo in frozen (or steaming) box cars from Salonika to Auschwitz. My actual train time to Krakow took about three days.

There was no Dr. Mengele at the funnel's end, waving a finger of life or death.

Governments have discovered other madnesses to occupy latter-day sophistications. Overkill capabilities.

A huge network of trackage collected the box cars near Vienna for transfer to the manufacturing plants in Poland. The famous European tracks from Drancy to Vienna or from Salonika to Vienna fed the northward funnel.

Nowhere were these tracks bombed by either the Western Powers or the Russians. Adolf Eichmann was not inhibited in his program of human logistics.

I purchase yet another bottle of mineral water as I board the train in Vienna for the Chopin Express run to Krakow. The tab for this water is a dollar. Two pears, at seventy cents each, would round out a bread and cheese breakfast about twelve hours later as the train would enter Poland.

This is a German car on the Chopin run, and spanking clean. Ample toilet paper in the WCs. The rhythm of the train's wheels still hammer away, but now at a higher pitch. I stretch out on one of the wide seats of the compartment, only to have the train stop at the Austrian border for the inevitable passport check.

Soon they'll repeat the process as we enter Czechoslovakia.

The Czech border official is a surly one. He wants $12 from each passenger—in cash. Travelers checks, naturally, won't do. He's about to toss me off the train when I finally come up with the cold cash. The money's for a Czech visa. "But I am not getting off in Czechoslovakia," I tell him (he speaks English). He shrugs.

Remind me never to visit Czechoslovakia. The SOB!

During the ride to the Polish border, I scan some notes from a friend, Leo Bach, who had lived in Krakow and was taken prisoner there by the Germans at age fourteen. By audacity and a will to survive, he managed to convince them of his skill as a technician. He was moved from camp to camp—a man-child confronting the swastika.

Leo's crude map is marked with these notations:

"This is the area of Krakow where the Germans established the Ghetto in March, 1941. The Nazis issued a decree that all Jews to the third generation must move into this Ghetto—or out of Krakow—by March 20, 1941. (I don't remember the exact date, but I think it was the 20th.) Any Jew found living in the town after that date would be shot. Any non-Jew giving aid or shelter to a Jew would also be shot."

At another section of the map:

"The small square where I indicate No. 4 is a small market-place known as Plac Zgody (Place of Agreement)—this was part of the Ghetto. In 1942, either in July or August (I don't remember exactly) several dozen Jewish people were murdered there—shot or clubbed to death by the Nazis, aided by the Polish police. There was a mass deportation of Jews to the death camps and those who resisted were dragged out of their apartments, clubbed and shot at."

At notation No. 5 on the map:

"This is the area where Concentration Camp Plaszow was located. Originally it was a new Jewish cemetery that was opened a few years before the war. The Nazis established a concentration camp there at the beginning of 1943. They removed all the gravestones and constructed barracks there to house prisoners.

"Commandant of the camp was SS Col. Amon Goet. He was an Austrian-born Nazi. (His name perhaps could have been Goette). He was a brutal murderer who committed many atrocities there. He had several SS officers as aides and several hundred uniformed Ukrainians and Latvians (volunteers!) to guard the camp. They were armed with all kinds of weapons, and equally brutal as the commandant."

A personal footnote from my friend reads:

"Where I indicated No. 5 (with relation to the entrance to Plaszow) there is a hill. On top of the hill there is a depression of perhaps thirty or forty feet in depth, about 100 feet across. There, hundreds of people were shot and buried in 1943.

"I was imprisoned there from June until mid-November 1943 and I remember that every few days a group of perhaps twenty or thirty people were escorted by armed Ukrainian guards and SS officers (sometimes by the commandant himself) to the top of the hill, where they were forced to undress. They were shot to death—in the nude.

"Who the victims were, I don't know exactly. According to the camp gossip, the victims were Jewish people who were discovered hiding somewhere in the Aryan world.

"Apparently the victims were discovered by the Gestapo agents or through Polish informers. Among the victims I remember seeing men, women and children of all ages.

"My brother, age fourteen, was shot there in November, 1943, after he was discovered by Polish informers and delivered by them to the Polish police who in turn delivered him to the Nazis."

*   *   *

Leaving Czechoslovakia is a simple matter of obtaining an exit stamp on my twelve-buck visa. The train moves on a bit and shudders to a halt. We are now in Poland.

(The box cars in transit to the death camps had no annoyance by border guards. Dr. Mengele was awaiting them at the end of the line—to wave a finger right or left: life or death. It was hardly life.)

A young Polish border girl attendant enters the compartment at about 3 a.m. to inspect a multitude of documents which I had obtained prior to launching this less than spectacular holiday abroad. I had deposited several hundred dollars with the Polish government, which would be exchanged for me into Polish zlotys upon arrival in Poland. This, to stop Americans from trading dollars on the black market.

The girl attendant counts out thirty two zlotys for each dollar I'd deposited with Polish representatives in the United States. On the black market, dollars are exchanged for 150 zlotys each. But I would have none of this. I must make it all the way at the official rate of exhange. A hardship, when the hotels such as the Krakowia charge at the rate of $46 a night for a tiny closet-like room.

The Chopin Express moves on, through an awakening landscape as dawn finally dawns on us. Breakfast as planned. There is hard-life farming in evidence everywhere, a myriad of rivers, forests—a soft rain is falling; we pass commuter trains being packed with riders to Warsaw; we pass freight yards and the inevitable box cars.

We pull into a depot.

There's a huge sign at the depot giving the city's name as Krakow. A porter takes my luggage to a taxi lineup outside. I rush back to shoot a picture of the Krakow sign.

As I walk back to the taxi stand, a plainclothes officer comes up and says: "It is forbidden to take pictures of railroads in Poland."

"Gosh, I'm sorry. All I shot was the sign."

"You must remember in the future," he said, walking back into the depot.

Big Brother was watching me?

But it could have become sticky, and I was grateful.

The taxi takes me, expensively, to the Hotel Francesca. I find out that I could have carried the bags a few hundered feet to the hotel. Communism in action.

12

There is no room available at the inn—the Francesca. Would I consider the deluxe Krakowia?

Would I not, for a hot shower?

But first I must visit the office of the U.S. Consulate General nearby. I had written in advance to meet with Consul General Nuel Logan Pazdral about details I might need for this travelogue. He turned out to be a marvelous gent from California. Graduate of Stanford. A newsman, too. Worked as a stringer for the McClatchy papers, for whom I also occasionally write.

Would I come to dinner at his home?

His wife is Jewish and is taking correspondence courses in Jewish studies from America.

I hadn't had a decent meal since leaving Israel. God bless America!

Back to the Francesca to gather up my luggage, I make it to the Krakowia where I am amazed at the tiny cell-like size of my "deluxe" room. Hot bath helped (no showers) and soon I am downstairs arranging for a room at the Hotel Bristol in Warsaw for the next night (half the cost of the Krakowia) and a driver to take me to Auschwitz in the morning.

The balance of this day I intend to explore important points on the map given to me by my friend.

A tram takes me to the Kazimierz Quarter, the old Jewish section of Krakow with its multitude of Jewish Synagogues and *yeshivot* (schools)—now empty or used as warehouses or apartments.

The German and his henchmen had done a savage job on Jewish institutions throughout Poland. This is a land that contained 3.5 million Jews prior to the Nazi invasion. They constituted 10 percent of all the people of Poland and made up 40 percent of life in the cities. An imprint of a thousand-year history!

The savagery of the German in going about the task of the "Final Solution" is evident in the elimination of most of the Jews of Europe. But there were moments enough, for them, to plunder treasured houses of worship, ancient schools and the thousand-year artistry of a people.

Plundered was Krakow's Alte Shul, built in the fourteenth century—the oldest remaining Synagogue in the land.

Nearby, on the same square, is the 16th century Remo Synagogue, the tiny house of worship which alone serves the needs of the several hundred Jews still living in Krakow.

The Alte Shul was declared a national monument by the Polish government and has been restored. I am told that a Jewish museum is contained inside but no visitors are allowed.

Rabbi Earl Vinecour, in his book, *The Final Chapter,* notes that the Alte Shul had "played a prominent role in the national history of Poland."

"In the course of the various insurrections against foreign domination, patriotic speeches had been given in its sanctuary urging Jews and Poles to unite in defense of their common homeland," he writes.

Vinecour points out that Jews fought for Poland's independence with ferocious bravery. In the 18th century, "Poland was partitioned by her neighbors. During that period, many Jews combined forces with Polish patriots to free their country from foreign domination."

"One of those Jews," the author writes, "Colonel Berek Joselewicz, became a Polish national hero fighting with the legendary Tadeusz Kosciuszko, who later joined the revolutionary army of George Washington in America's struggle for independence."

Then, says Vinecour, Kosciuszko wrote: "The Jews have proven to the world that when the welfare of humanity is at stake, they know not how to spare their lives."

Less than two hundred years later, a Poland whipped into frenzy against the Jews by the Church on the one hand and Nazi invaders on the other gave up her Jews to the slaughterers. For loaves of bread.

I was barred from entering the Remo Synagogue also. But I managed to visit the ancient cemetery to the rear of the Synagogue, Poland's oldest Jewish burial ground. Vinecour notes that the only tombstone to survive the war here, totally unimpaired, was that of Rabbi Moses Isserles.

A tall iron fence surrounds the sage's burial site and probably inhibited its destruction. Most of the rest of the small cemetery has been restored with the financial assistance of America's Joint Distribution Committee.

My friend Leo Bach told me: "My mother's parents are buried there, and three of her sisters."

Vinecour notes that the cemetery contains the remains of prominent Jews who served not only the cause of Jewish survival, but the people and kings of Poland generally.

While browsing inside the Remo Synagogue, wrote Vinecour, "I came across trunks full of Torah Scrolls and literally thousands of decaying books."

"Take them to America," one old man said to him. But

another quickly cut in: "The government won't let them out even if they rot in Poland!"

Once, an estimated 75,000 Jews lived in Krakow. Talking with the survivors, I detected a sense of shame among some that they were still living there. Many are reduced to begging from Jewish visitors from abroad.

Jewish life in Krakow is dead.

I wander away from the area of the Remo Synagogue to visit the Temple, an imposing baroque structure built in the 1920s to serve the richer Jews of Krakow. I am allowed inside by the caretaker and am impressed with the structure's stained glass windows and iron artistry surrounding the Ark. In my mind's eye I could see the accomplished men of Krakow in prayer at the community's most elegant Synagogue; and the grand ladies, dressed in their finest, for Shabbat.

The caretaker lives in what was once the daily chapel for prayer. The Temple of Krakow—now a monument to incredible disturbances of the minds of men.

* * *

It starts to rain and I hasten toward the tram. But as suddenly, the rain stops and I cross the car tracks, just wandering. I come upon another Jewish cemetery and am aghast to find broken gravestones that are now cemented into a cone-shaped monument. Walls along pathways of the cemetery are built of these broken headstones. There are no families left to cry havoc.

I turn back to the tram and make it to the Krakowia, chilled and shaken.

At eight o'clock I am downstairs where Consul General Nuel Pazdral is already waiting beside his spanking new white Plymouth. We drive to his home.

I am hardly prepared for elegant dress on travels such as

this. I try to cover my being out of dress by glib small talk. The forced smiles of my hosts and another couple that had just driven down from Warsaw turn my small talk into shambles.

Mrs. Pazdral is charming. I give her one of my books of poetry and she is genuinely happy to receive it.

"You know, this is the former home of Pieter Menten," she says.

It is an impressive home, indeed the kind a Nazi collector of art works might choose as his own. After all, he was a known dealer in the arts. He could choose any home that was liberated from the Jews.

Nuel knew a friend of mine in the Foreign Service, Chet Opal, who had worked with me in Chicago at the City News Bureau. Last I heard, Chet was assigned to the American embassy in Amman, Jordan.

It was a great dinner after sumptuous meals of bread, cheese and mineral water that had marked my travels so far.

Nuel said he would call Orbis, the Polish travel agency, to arrange for a certain driver who was very familiar with the areas of Jewish history to drive me to Auschwitz in the morning.

"I hope he will also be able to take me to Plaszow, the concentration camp where my friend's brother was shot," I said.

Nuel brings out a large map of the area and sees there is a road leading from Plaszow to Auschwitz—round about, but it can be done.

It was a lovely evening. And Mrs. Pazdral's pie was the greatest. Indeed, memorable.

13

Weeping Stones

Even the stones grieve
at Plaszow
beside the cavern in the earth's
mass grave that swallowed
martyred memories
a bullet riddled heartbreak ago.

Grieve, tall stones
shed your granite tears
upon the tangled brush
and shattered dreams.

For here, oh somewhere
here, I hear the soulful cry
of a boy
brother of a friend.

Krakow, August 24, 1978

77

The very seasoned guide who was assigned to take me to Auschwitz said he once heard about Plaszow. Knew its general direction. But, since nobody goes there—didn't exactly know its location.

The plan was to visit Plaszow, proceed to Auschwitz, light a candle at the destroyed gas chambers, then have the driver drop me off at the railroad station for the trip to Warsaw. I wanted very much to attend Sabbath services that evening at Warsaw's only Synagogue. It was a full day's task I had laid out.

The eerie thought grabbed me: what traveler in human experience would have planned such a day?

Plaszow, to recite Kaddish for the brother of my friend, at the site of the ravine of death which was now a mystery in Krakow.

Auschwitz, perhaps to hear the cry of a child upon a passing, withering wind: where the worst thing that ever happened, happened. I must listen for the cry of that child—that his tears are not alone.

Then, to sigh in gratitude to the memory of Oskar Schindler, the Nazi bureaucrat who was assigned to a section of Plaszow as overseer of a German factory. Oskar Schindler—for whom a tree grows on the Mountain of Remembrance in Israel. Oh, there are so few trees along the pathway of the Righteous Gentiles!

Briefly, the Schindler story. It was written for major film production by Metro-Goldwyn-Mayer, then shelved.

Aghast at what he saw of German and Polish inhumanity, Oskar Schindler assembled his factory's 1,300 Jews and developed a plan of work at Plaszow that would make literally nothing. Whatever tasks were assigned to the Schindler factory fell flat: the machines created wrong fittings and Schindler became a master at finding where the Gestapo bones were buried. Nobody dared point a finger in the direction of the Schindler factory.

Somehow, Oskar Schindler found food for his workers. When a number of wives of Schindler's Jews were taken to Auschwitz for extermination, he hurried to the huge camp and arranged their release.

As war turned into disaster for the Germans, the Schindler factory was moved from place to place.

Oskar Schindler remained with his 1,300 Jews "until five minutes before midnight," according to Leopold Page, who was one of the Schindler Jews and who devoted his life to helping Schindler in his final days.

Five minutes after Schindler left his Jews, the Russians broke through the German lines and the Jews were saved. Schindler cautioned his Jews not to exhibit savagery to the Germans, their captors, even though they had been dehumanized for so long.

The good German!

*   *   *

But how to find Plaszow?

Our car drives fifteen kilometers to where the driver was told the camp existed. Two old men, riding a horse-drawn cart, tell the driver that there is some mistake. No Plaszow camp for Jews was ever in the area. But they recall a huge monument some kilometers back and off to the left—could that be Plaszow?

In the countryside we come upon an enormous granite memorial of four tall figures, their heads starkly bowed in grief. The memorial stands upon a hill overlooking a ravine—exactly as described by my friend.

It is a long pathway to the crest of the hill and to the memorial. An overwhelming sadness surges through me as I approach the monument. It is difficult to look down into the cavern. I recite the Hebrew prayer for the dead. As I recite it, my voice rises and rises and rises. Soon I am shouting the prayer across the ravine.

There is a small stone marker nearby, inscribed in Polish. Then back to the car. We drive a direct road to the house which apparently was the commandant's headquarters. The commandant was known to take delight in shooting Jewish slave workers walking nearby. His savage sadism was fed when his snarling dog would tear a Jew to pieces.

This was the German camp at Plaszow. Other than the monument and the house of the commandant, nothing remains of the camp. The barracks are gone; the electrified barbed wire is gone. If there ever was a Jewish cemetery here, only the wild grasses know.

There is deathly silence hovering over these fields.

We drive to Auschwitz.

*   *   *

There is a shorter way to Oswiecim from Krakow. By that

route it is about thirty miles. From Plaszow, we circle about from the north; it is a considerably longer distance.

It is August in the Poland countryside. Farmers stack their hay in small bundles. Men and women are in the fields with scythes, cutting hay in wide swings of their arms. They cut so pathetically little amounts of hay. One tractor could do wonders for a dozen farmers.

We drive past an idyllic village with wrought iron fences, each section of fence painted another pastel color. A horse-drawn wagon passes, heavily laden with hay. A pastoral setting to inspire Gypsy violinists. Where are the Gypsies? Where are the musicians? I hum a Viennese waltz.

The Chopin Express went on to Warsaw from Krakow—but massive tracks branched off directly to Oswiecim from Krakow. We somehow avoid the tracks coming to this small Polish town from the north. But these were among the busiest tracks in all of Europe when they were under the control of the German.

There were four camps that comprised the huge Auschwitz complex in the days of madness.

Birkenau was the most heinous in history—the section of Auschwitz where men, women and children were selected for extermination.

The able-bodied men were marched under a huge iron sign with the German words *Arbeit Macht Frei*—"Labor Makes One Free."

Here, beside the sign, some of the great musicians of Europe were playing delightful Viennese waltzes (to their own heartbreak). The able-bodied inmates would be assigned to barracks and to work details hearing music!

The slave labor, for the most part, would be assigned to the infamous I.G. Farben chemical plant—an operation so huge that it consumed more electricity than the entire city of Berlin.

Later, as Farben overseers became unhappy with the work process as devised by the German SS, the great petrochemical company set up its own concentration camp nearby, to gain better control over its slave laborers.

It's all delineated in the Joseph Borkin book on Farben, *The Crime and Punishment of I.G. Farben.*

Still driving toward Oswiecim, I scan a scene of great beauty: a mother and daughter raking straw in front of their home, wearing babushkas. A tour bus is now in front of us. We cross some railroad tracks, the back tracks leading away from Auschwitz. Now we come upon the village of Kwaczata, a tiny crossroads town containing a tavern as its center of attraction. Then the field in front of a larger town, Bobice. We cross the Vistula River (once a Jewish river to the sea—so many Jewish villages bordered the Vistula); past a forest of tall trees and brush (they flushed Jews out of this forest and returned them to the German for their loaves of bread); past Zarki, a new suburb of Auschwitz.

My God! Auschwitz has become a Disneyland for Poland—a tourist attraction!

Oswiecim seems a long way away, somehow. But now the roadsign points left. It's a busy industrial town; we cross an abundance of railroad tracks, past the town's train depot and an array of box cars, and into a huge parking area.

Auschwitz.

The parking area is filled almost to capacity with tour buses, many from the Soviet Union.

I am ushered into a small cinema which describes the concept of Auschwitz: as a manufacturing camp, a holding camp and a death camp. Mostly death.

The film in English has a Soviet slant. The Soviets, of course, won the war. There is only passing reference to the Jews—three and a half million of whom lost their lives here. The victims, it seems, were Poles, Hungarians, Russians, Greeks.

I join an English-speaking tour; the guide is a Polish woman who tells how the fascists kept meticulous records of those who were murdered here. I inform her that I saw the records on a previous trip through the "museum" (oh, the barracks are now a huge museum and visitors come to see the Grand Canyon, Poland's great national attraction).

"Where are the records?" I ask. "They were out in the open, in 1961." The guide glares at me.

The hallways of the barracks are lined with photographs of young victims of the Nazis. None of their names is Jewish. The dignity (or indignity) of being listed in death was denied to Jewish victims. Only Christian victims appear to have been recorded. Jews were subhuman—faceless, nameless.

We are shown the usual collections of macabre artifacts salvaged from the Nazis: mounds of hair, false teeth, crutches, shoes. The suitcases told the story, however. Each had a name painted on its side. Almost all the names were Jewish! At one case there is a display of Jewish prayer shawls. Here the guide makes the first reference to Jewish victims.

These barracks were of brick—the holding area for workers who would be forced to run (exhausted, without food) to the Farben plant four miles away. If they fell by the wayside, finish.

I try to enter a "Jewish Pavilion" which was intended to tell the martyrdom here of the Jewish people. The guide had rushed the group past the pavilion. A Russian girl at the Jewish pavilion says I may not enter. "People are working inside," she insists.

My driver takes me to the Birkenau section of Auschwitz, some miles distant. The tracks lead right through a rural looking train depot, and on past a number of wooden barracks to the right.

The driver parks his car in a lot containing several buses. Near the entrance to Birkenau, vendors sell ice cream cones to the visitors. Everybody is in a happy mood. On holiday, after all.

The barracks to the right were holding facilities for women and children. As needed to keep the fires burning, the victims would be marched half a mile to the shower rooms, the German macabre description for gas chambers, where Jews would inhale Zyklon B gas. Moments later they would be incinerated, their ashes rising through a number of tall chimneys to fertilize the memories of Poland.

O those chimneys!

There are three crematoria. It is not necessary to visit all. I find it difficult enough to visit one—its roof blown to a contortion of shattered reinforced concrete. The German tried to erase his infamy when Allied forces moved in from all sides.

I don my prayer shawl and *tfillin* and recite morning prayers.

I light a candle which I had brought from Israel, placed upon a piece of stone blown from the gas chamber. Again I recite the *Kaddish*—again my voice rises across a macabre scene. A number of other visitors hear me and watch me.

"Hear oh Israel, the Lord our God, the Lord is One!"

I recite the single doctrine of the Jewish faith. Then remove my prayer shawl and *tfillin.*

I walk to a huge stone plaza and monument nearby, which tells in many languages (including Yiddish and Hebrew) what the fascist had done. That Jews of Europe were the singular target of the madness is not mentioned in any of the languages. The Holocaust was a Jewish Holocaust. That others also died in it was incidental to the German intent.

Nearby, the tracks end directly in front of the monument. These are the tracks that led from Drancy in France and Salonika in Greece to a long siding, here, at Birkenau.

Jewish victims would be "selected" by the waving of a German finger playing God. Who for life; who for death.

I stare at the tracks a long, bitter time.

Will there ever be another Final Solution, another Heydrich, another Eichmann?

Will there ever be another Hitler?

I walk away to join my driver for another pastoral ride through the Polish countryside and the train to Warsaw.

I notice that around Auschwitz, the countryside is utterly fertile.

15

In the dining room of the Krakow train station, I am carefully avoided by the waitress. She speaks no English. My Polish is less than nil. I have two hours for the train to Warsaw and suddenly realize I hadn't eaten all day.

A waiter who assumes the air of possessing an exquisite command of English finally approaches my table and says: "What you want? Soup? Weel?"

God love him, it is hard to keep from laughing. It's like the time at the Maria Isabella Sheraton in Mexico City; scanning the menu, I came upon a curious item: "New Scotland Salmon." That's for me. I explained to another guest: "They really mean Nova Scotia lox." Oh.

I notice one American is brave and orders the soup and "weel". Turns out to be a thin vegetable-type soup and a leathery veal cutlet. I order the national drink of Poland (or so it seems to those riding the rails of the country)—Pepsi. Must be a national monopoly. That, and vodka.

I notice that bravery ends after a few tastes of the soup and a sliver of "weel". I am determined to find a market near the station and now I brave the uncharted streets of Krakow. A loaf of black bread, a chunk of cheese and a few apples would be very welcome indeed.

I pass a large hostel set aside for Russian visitors. The Russians are busy photographing themselves. They're on holiday—among the groups that visit the museums of Auschwitz. I cross a large street and join a queue for bread at a small market. Then, a queue for cheese. Then a queue for fruit. The apples are small and pretty bad. But peelable.

Seated on a bench at the train station, using a huge folding knife I had purchased in Istanbul, I slice hunks of bread and chunks of cheese and peel a couple of apples and enjoy—beside the tracks that would take me soon to Warsaw. Oh, these tracks have a sudden impact on me. Soon it becomes hard to swallow.

The train pulls along and I find I must carry my luggage a considerable distance to the rear of the train—to the car to which I was assigned. Occasionally in my travels I'd come upon a porter. Somewhat.

It would take about four hours to Warsaw. Too late for evening services. Darkness is descending, and so is a stiff rain. We cross a number of large rivers and then the train burrows underground to emerge inside a huge, new train terminal.

No porters again. I find a luggage cart and make it to the taxi stand. Another long queue. After half an hour, partially protected from the rain by an overhang, but adequately chilled, a taxi takes me to the Bristol Hotel. There are some guides in Warsaw who will tell you that pianist Jan Paderewski, as President of Poland, used the Bristol as his palace. Others say that the Bristol is where he entertained guests such as Herbert Hoover and other heads of state. Not exactly his palace.

I found the Bristol to be a seedy hostelry with old world charm, its lift a century old relic which admitted passengers through one door and evicted them through another. And when the elevator operator was drunk (as he most often appeared to be) it was a wild ride to the second floor.

I was ushered into a huge, high-ceilinged room with a large sleeping alcove to the side, a tub that appeared twelve feet long, give or take a stretch, a refrigerator, huge desk and a wide-bench reclining couch. Identical room to one I occupied at the National Hotel in Moscow, on Red Square. My impression is that the Bristol may be a direct copy of the Moscow hostelry.

And yes, the television worked. Not that I could understand even one unmentionable word. They had a way of blocking out the English dialogue on American westerns and a narrator would tell the story in Polish, dialogue and all.

Dined in the hotel restaurant, which featured an American-type dance band with a girl singer belting out rock songs in Polish. After a bit I gave up and fled to my room. It was all too incongruous.

Early, Sabbath morning, I brave a sudden rainstorm that sweeps Warsaw and head for the only Synagogue still open in the city—the Nozik Shul, one of the three Synagogues in Poland designated as national shrines.

During a halt to the rain, I walk into a large square near the Intercontinental Victoria Hotel and observe soldiers standing stiffly at attention. It is the tomb of Poland's Unknown Soldier. Nearby are two elderly people, a woman and a man. I say to them one word, in the sound of a question: "Synagoga?" — "Plac Grzybowski."

The man suddenly speaks rapidly to the woman, drawing an imaginary map on the sidewalk with his cane.

"Come with me," says the woman, in perfect English.

Spry as hell, easily seventy years old, she leads me swiftly toward a main street. I have difficulty keeping pace.

At a busy intersection, she inquires in Polish of another man for directions to Plac Grzybowski. He waves his hand in the direction of a large Catholic church. The woman leads and I follow. "Your don't look like a Jew," she finally says. "What does a Jew look like?" I ask. "Jewish," she says. We come to a monument in this city of monuments. She asks directions of another elderly woman who had been there (Here? Was this the ghetto?) when this was the city of tears.

My guide, a tiny grey-haired woman, listens to the other woman intently, then informs me: "She says that at All Saints Church, across the street, a priest rescued a Jewish man named Hirshfeld and his family. He was a well-known writer and doctor."

We cross to the church. "It may or may not be true," says my guide. "That's what we must find out."

How did she learn her English? "My husband was a musician and we went to New York for a time."

Then she says: "My sister married a Jew. When my husband died, we told the Germans that her husband was my husband. We gave him a Polish name."

Two Polish sisters had saved a Jew! Perhaps more, but I must not ask. Her eyes were tearing. We come to the church and find its administrative office. Father Rzewnicki is at the desk. He speaks English, but somewhat haltingly.

I ask about a Jewish doctor who may have been saved by the priest during the war.

"It's all in the chronicles," he says. "I will show you. But first, let us go to the tower."

We are led up many flights of steps to a large loft, used perhaps by a choir. "This is where the family lived all through the war," says Father Rzewnicki.

It is a barren room. A table. Two chairs. Bare walls. I think of the Annex of Anne Frank. Except there was fighting going on throughout Warsaw. The Ghetto was demolished. The priest says the church was struck by many bombs and much of it was destroyed. Have I come upon another act of bravery by the Polish people? Indeed, there must have been many such acts of bravery.

There may have been many such acts of bravery in Spain!

We descend the stairs to the main church. The priest and the woman genuflect and cross themselves. It is the Jewish Sabbath and here I am in a church—on the trail of a story of Catholic bravery and the rescue of an eminent Jew.

I recall the words of Gideon Hausner at the Eichmann trial: one may have opinions, but one must be fair.

The priest leads us to a wall at the side of the main church sanctuary. Here are enlarged offset prints of statements by a Dr. Ludwig Hirszfeld.

My woman guide offers to translate.

"In August 1941 we got our own flat in the Parish House of the All Saints Church. Father Godlewski was our protector. When I say this name, I am deeply moved." It was signed, "Prof. Hirszfeld, M.D."

The words were read over Polish television, the document states.

I am deeply moved and the woman leads me by the arm out of the church. At the doorway she turns, genuflects and crosses herself again.

We leave the church and across the street is Plac Grzy-bowski. To the right is a large modern building which houses the Kaminska Yiddish Theater and the weekly Yiddish news-paper, *Folks-Sztyme,* "the People's Voice."

(I suddenly recall that it was the *Folks-Sztyme* which printed the Khrushchev "cult of the personality" speech which stripped Stalin of his niche in Russian history. The speech told how scores of Yiddish writers and poets had been slain by a mad-dened Soviet dictator. My newspaper, *Heritage*, obtained the story from Adolph Held and Harry Lang, of the Jewish Labor Committee, back in 1954. *Folks-Sztyme* proved them right two weeks later.)

I must visit the *Folks-Sztyme's* editor. Later. Later.

My guide takes me into a side pathway, and there we come upon the Nozik Shul, hidden from the main street, a deplorable building—a Polish national shrine?

A number of old men hover about the Synagogue's entrance.

"These people look like Jews, that's why I knew we were in the right place," says the woman.

(Jews must look like beggars? With long noses? God love this brave woman. We are all social animals and react to triggers of a world about us. We all contain elements of bigotry, as we may also contain seeds of greatness. Convolutions and convulsions of feelings whirl within us all.)

She takes my hand. I want very much to plant a kiss upon her cheek. She smiles warmly to me. "I leave you with your people," she says, turns, and disappears. I watch her turning from the pathway of the Synagogue and out of view.

16

The Jews of Poland in front of the Synagogue surround me.

Each professes a different catastrophic ailment, for which, for each, the prescription is the same: American dollars.

The trouble with the illnesses and the cure is that I had been to this Synagogue in 1966 when, for the first time, I had met these same fakirs. From a 1966 community of about 22,000 Polish Jews—there were now, twelve years later, only 4,000 left. It was sad to watch the moochers scurrying to make a fast buck off American sorrows in Warsaw. Sad, and revolting.

This is the Poland of great Talmudic scholars. This is the Poland of Yud Lamed Peretz, of Mendele Mocher Sforim, of Sholom Aleichem. Indeed, of Nobel Laureate Isaac Bashevis Singer.

Hundreds of Jewish schools abounded. Klezmers were tooting their melancholy tunes of a people for whom there was one communal ideal: learning. (How did they dare, in Berlin, to manufacture that ideal to death!)

In the thousands, Jews offered their lives to Germany in the first World War. Rabbi Jacob Sonderling, one of Germany's top

Jewish chaplains in that war, often told me how Jewish genius kept German guns blazing: the Haber process alone ought to have merited a nation's gratitude. The Haber process for the manufacture of ammonia ultimately created the I.G. Farben industries—which operated one of the four slave camps at Auschwitz, a Hitlerian era hence.

At least Albert Einstein was saved. And Leo Szilard. And Edward Teller. The prime level Jewish scientists who managed to escape the net of the Final Solution ultimately helped assure the downfall of the Thousand Year Reich.

These were the thoughts that were with me as I entered the barren, shabby Nozik Shul—the last one remaining in Warsaw. A national Polish monument.

Strangely, I hear young voices.

Young voices in the Nozik Shul?

Have young people finally emerged from the recesses of Warsaw to rekindle the Sabbath in Poland?

But I know there are no children left to be B'nai Mitzvah in Warsaw. There are no ceremonial circumcisions. There are no Jewish babies born in Warsaw—a city that was home to 600,000 Jews only a bitter memory ago.

I find myself surrounded by 25 American students—boys and girls who are concluding Sabbath prayers with song. An Oneg Shabbat.

I felt a sudden guilt: I had gone to a church on the Sabbath to trace down a story and had missed prayers with these young people. Their leader, Michael Rosen, from New York, explains they are part of a large Bnei Akiva group on its way to Israel for a year of study. All are of upper high school age. This group had decided to come to Poland on a "Holocaust Journey," en route to Israel.

The leader introduces me to his mother, Mrs. Sara Rosen, who was born in Krakow and had miraculously fled a death camp to somehow escape to the West. Her sister died at Auschwitz.

"Why are you in Poland?" she asks.

I tell her my plans for this book. "I don't know if I have the heart and eyes to write the book. The project is simple but enormous."

"It will be a good book," she says.

She is suddenly the newsperson: "Was your family from Poland?"

"My father was born in Konin," I say. "I hope to visit there in a few days."

"What was the family name?"

"Dobrzinski—they assumed the Polish name. The family name was originally Abarbanel."

"What? Dobrzinski? We have a girl in our group with a similar name."

I suddenly freeze. I had made many attempts to find even a single survivor of my family in Konin.

Mrs. Rosen takes me to the girl. Alas, no. Her father came from Warsaw. The names are indeed somewhat similar. But there it ends. Again.

Outside it is now raining heavily. The students invite me back to evening services. There will be a *Shalleh Shudes* and *Havdallah*—an evening meal of song and prayer followed by the awesome and beautiful ceremony for ushering out the Sabbath. Also, noted Polish author, Szymon Datner, would be there to speak to the students.

I promise to return, push my way into the rain—it had softened somewhat—and find myself surrounded again by the seekers of American dollars. I brush them aside. Suddenly a pleasant old man walks briskly to my side as we leave the Synagogue area. He says:

"Zey zainen hooliganen. Gib zey nicht ein grosh!"

"They are hooligans. Don't give them even a grosh (penny)."

17

Szymon Datner—the final sage of Poland.

At the suggestion of Norman Melnick of the San Francisco *Examiner*, who had spent many weeks in Poland researching conditions of Polish Jewry for a series in his newspaper, I telephoned Szymon Datner.

I asked whether he would mind if I taped his address to the American students at *Shalleh Shudes.* He didn't mind, indeed, welcomed the thought. And despite a cold wind and rain, protected somewhat by a torn umbrella, I found my way through the Warsaw darkness to the Nozik Shul, walking through pockets of water that had become a moat around the Synagogue.

The evening services were begun by the students in semi-glow and darkness. There was an occasional light bulb burning and candles on a long table laden with twisted *challeh,* some tomatoes, some cucumbers, *gefilte* fish brought from America in cans—and vodka.

This was the splendor of a Sabbath repast in Warsaw's only

Synagogue. The Sabbath would be ushered out in bleak auster-ity. But with song. Oh, the songs the students sang: one upon the other, like an endless flow of blood through their Jewish hearts.

Suddenly, there was silence. A short, aged man, whom I spotted in fervent prayer earlier, was given the place of honor at the "banquet" table. I was seated at the opposite end of the table, beside a small, hunchbacked man who emerged as the loudest of the Warsaw Jews, his voice more than heavily inspired by the vodka.

But now there was silence. We awaited the lecture of the last sage of Warsaw, Szymon Datner.

(I made no effort to pry his story: why did he remain in Poland when other survivors fled? The fact that he was here is sorrow enough, drama enough. Do I dare to pour acid on the wounds? I was about to listen to his words and I didn't under-stand a word of Hebrew!)

Rachel Tugend offers this tape translation. Rachel had fought in 1948 in Jersualem for the rebirth of Israel out of these ashes of Poland. Rachel understood. Every heartthrob of the voice on tape.

"We see young faces here, faces of young people. . ."

Rav Datner's voice was low on the tape, barely audible.

I recall his face flushed with remembrances. A *Shalleh Shudes* in a shabby Synagogue! Unwashed table linen. Shad-ows of tragedy staring down from crevices of a House of Worship where once a community of dignified Jews would come for a Sabbath in warmth, filled with *kavanah.* Dedication. Holiness.

"We have not had the privilege of seeing any young people here in Warsaw for a very long time. It was not unusual, thirty-five years ago, to see many young people like you at our Sabbath Table.

"Then, we had our youth. Then, we numbered three and a half million Jews in Poland. Today, we don't even know exactly how may Jews are still alive in Poland. Some say four or five thousand. The optimists say about ten thousand.

"This is what is left for us out of three and a half million who were here before the Nazis destroyed eight to nine hundred Jewish centers of life in this country.

"Of the Jewish population we had at that time, less than half a million managed to get out. Most went to Israel. Some to the United States. The rest to other parts of the world.

"I was saved. Somehow the Jewish world was saved. Today, Jews of the world number about fourteen million. . ."

His voice was rising as the statistics flowed.

"The Holocaust of the German was not the only one the Jews went through. We pray it will be the last one.

"With this as background, it is most important that we have the State of Israel. This is a pearl that attracts all of world Jewry. It will not eliminate completely, nor solve all the problems of Jews in the Diaspora. But it gives us hope for the future.

"By going to Israel to study, you make a great contribution. When I see a group of young people like you who live under the best conditions in the world—and you choose to move from a place of safety to a state where there are dangers (and I pray you will be spared from any danger)—when I see what you are choosing, I bow my head to you and such a youth.

"It is mine to congratulate you, Bnei Akiba, who know how to combine worldly culture and our Jewish tradition. You are the guarantee of the continued existence of the Jewish people.

"When you get to Israel, you will be coming from the site of the most terrible catastrophe that ever befell a people—a catastrophe that is not equaled in any event in our history beside the destruction of our First and Second Temples.

"Take with you to Israel the greetings from the handful of Jews left in Poland. I charge you with two loves: the love of our people in Israel, and the love of our ancient homeland.

"Your are going to far away places. You left close family ties thousands of kilometers away. Remember that they miss you.

They will miss you. Write to them regularly. As you came in peace to Poland, leave in peace—remembering what you see here. Fulfill your duty in your *hachshara*—that your ties to your people and your homeland will be strengthened, a homeland that is constantly in danger."

* * *

Through the sorrowful words of Rav Datner, which I did not understand as he spoke them, a sense of prophecy emerged.

I wasn't alone to sense it.

Beside me stood a tall, rather handsome man, wearing fine American clothing. Was he Jewish? If there is a Polish Slavic face, it was upon him.

Rav Datner was far from finished.

"Throughout the generations there were always enemies who wanted to destroy us. But God—and we ourselves, with our youth—saves us from their hands. And so I must teach you a song I have written for this day.

"It has to do with the story in Samuel II, Chapter 3, which speaks of two captains in the time of King David. One was Joab, the other, Abner.

"Abner was slain by Joab and David cried that he and his kingdom were guiltless before the Lord. And at the end of the Chapter, David says, 'The Lord will reward the evildoer according to his wickedness.'

"These words were spoken 3,000 years ago. Only a handful of Nazis have been punished for their crimes. Most were not. But the Lord will reward the evildoer according to his wickedness."

That was the chant of a song that now filled the Nozik Shul.

Rav Datner would remind the students of an act of terror committed upon the Jews: Maalot, an El Al bus, a marketplace in Jerusalem; then the refrain—"The Lord will reward the evildoer according to his wickedness."

Suddenly it all ended and the loudest Jew in Warsaw began pouring vodka as from a pent-up fountain, consuming the tiny balls of *gefilte* fish along with chunks of *challeh* which he hadn't had in such abundance, perhaps, in decades. The tomatoes were unwashed? He wiped them on the dirty tablecloth. No matter. All the while, singing the traditional Sabbath songs, the *zmirot* hallowed for the Sabbath.

I felt a tug on my arm. The "American" was beside me saying how nice it was to see such a sight once again in Poland.

"Are you Jewish?" I asked.

No, he was a priest from America. Head of the Catholic Interethnic Council in Washington, D.C.

18

Rav Datner was smiling. I wondered when last he had smiled this special smile, that a thread of continuity of a people had come back oh so briefly to Warsaw. Nearby, of course, if one scrapes the soil, a scream might arise from where Jews fought in the Ghetto Warsaw.

But who will scrape the soil on a rain-swept night in Poland?

I asked the priest, Father Waclaw Zajaczkowski, if he had ever heard of Father Godlewski, former prelate of the All Saints Church across the street.

Father Zajaczkowski was suddenly silent. Stunned. How did I know of Godlewski?

"I was told he saved the life of Prof. Ludwik Hirszfeld."

The songs of the students and the handful of pious Jews at the evening service were mounting in crescendo as backdrop to a savage discussion: Jew and priest—in the Nozik Shul!

"Yes, I knew of Prof. Hirszfeld. He was an eminent hemotologist whose book will be translated soon into English. You must know that the Jews of Warsaw generally regarded Father Godlewski as a bitter anti-Semite."

(Hands were clapping to ancient Hebraic melodies. The hunchback with the enormous voice embraced each glass of vodka with zest.)

"Why?" was my inevitable question.

Because in those days before the war there were ten million Poles who wanted to leave the farms and come to the cities and make their way in commerce and industry. These were all in the hands of the Jews.

"When you competed in the city with a Jew, you were considered an anti-Semite. If somebody was a watchmaker and wanted to open a store in the city, Jews wouldn't help him. They wouldn't lend him the means."

"Do you mean that Father Godlewski filled the countryside with this garbage? That's incredible anti-Semitism!" I said.

Adding: "Did the Church lend a watchmaker the means of opening up a shop, say, in Lodz? And why were the Jews in the cities and towns? Because the Church played a documented role in keeping Jews off the land of Poland."

(Oh, how the chanting voices of the Shabbat swept the darkened corners of the shabby Synagogue.)

The role of the newsman is to report. But here I was, not as newsman but as a traveler through frightful memories.

"If Godlewski saved one Jew but spread his poison of hatred through Poland, anti-Semitism rests at the doorsteps of his church and the churches of Poland," I said.

"That's generalization," said Dr. Zajaczkowksi.

I persisted:

"Hatred of the Jews that swept Poland long before World War II had nothing to do with commerce and industry. It had to do with the unique quality of inventiveness that somehow marks the Jew. That's what they hated as they feared. And Godlewski fed the fires!"

Someone handed me a glass of vodka and a dirty tomato. I held on to these until the singing would end, very much later.

I suggested to the priest that there were millions of Poles who were emancipated from the rationale of hatred that spread like poisoned tentacles from the priesthoods of Poland. These brave Poles also died at Auschwitz and Majdanek. But the curious rationale of a Godlewski that would deprive a Jew of his right to till the soil and then of his job in the city—that was the heart of Polish anti-Semitism.

(We spoke into each other's ears—the crescendo of *zmirot* became so loud.)

"Well then," I said, "my father was born in Konin. He served in the Russian army during the Russian-Japanese War of 1905. Why did he leave for America? Because of the bitterness he found among the Polish people against the Jews. What commerce did the Jews control in the small towns of Poland, where families eked out livings by sewing rags? They called it survival. There was no King Casimir to offer protection to the Jews of Poland. If the Poles felt they were poor and the Jews were rich—why was I called *zhid!* on Claremont Avenue in Chicago by the Poles who lived in the nice apartments while we lived in a basement?"

I was pouring out my heart to a priest who had come to the Nozik Shul of a Shabbat night to join in the ancient *zmirot*. But then, neither of us could have predicted this encounter.

When I mentioned Claremont Avenue, the priest's eyes lit up.

"I lived in that neighborhood for more than 10 years," he said. "Chicago was a Polish town. The density of the Polish people in Chicago was incredible. It was there that I formulated the Catholic Interethnic Council."

(My heart went out to him. A righteous Gentile! There were so few.)

I told him my parents sold the daily *Dziennik Zwiazkowy Zgoda* and *Chicagoski* newpapers. I covered the police beats for the City News Bureau of Chicago at night. In the morning, I'd drive my father to the Polish newpaper offices to collect the day's papers which my father, mother and I would sell on newsstands outside the Crane Co. on South Kedzie Avenue.

Rain or shine; snow or heat. There was no protection from the elements other than a barrel of fire. The papers told of the Hitlerian tragedies in Poland.

Often, a story I'd covered the previous night would be

featured on page one of the English language dailies. On occasion, a story by my father would appear on page one of the Polish dailies. My father detected the direction of national life in Poland—he tried his best to head off the anti-Jewish implica- tions he was forced to sell at his newsstands. But it was sell these newspapers in an era of Depression, or starve.

The priest detected my sorrow, my reluctance to embarrass him—yet a compelling need to speak my mind as the chanting and hand-clapping continued.

He said: "These Poles, here in Poland during the Hitler years—they were ordinary people. They were not heroes. Who is a hero? How many heroes are there in the world? How many in America would be heroes in such a case?"

"They were heroes in Denmark when they saved the Jews," I suggested.

"Denmark was special. It was a show window for Hitler in Western Europe—to show how the Nazis handled their prison- ers with kindness.

"You must remember that the Jews of France were Frenchmen; in Germany, they were Germans. In Poland they remained Jews. Heinrich Heine describes the difference be- tween a Polish Jew and a German Jew. He said the Polish Jew is proud. A German Jew is trying to pass as a German."

Then he hit hard: "When it meant their lives to save a Jew, the Polish people were not heroes. My mother did it. We gave shelter to a Jewish woman and her child—Irene Franziak and her daughter. They are now living in Tel Aviv.

"No, the Poles were not heroes. But tell me, where *were* the heroes?"

While the singing and chanting and clapping swept the emptiness of the Nozik Shul, I felt to cry.

"The heroes," I said, "... they went up in smoke when the Germans found out. But history has a right to demand that no human being turn another over to the murderer for a loaf of bread. One who is fleeing naked in some Poland forest."

I persisted: "Humanity required a national sense of revulsion in Poland. Instead, Jews found an enormity of collaboration. Where was the Church, where were the voices of outrage in Rome? How many millions might have been spared such an outrage! And the Church would have been embraced by nobility."

The priest fell silent.

"And in Spain. The Church of Inquisition was directly culpable," I said.

Father Zajaczkowski reached deeply into his heart for answer: "The Church was misled by monarchs at the time."

I suggested that the reverse might also be true. But then, what is truth? Jesus was not alone on the cross of Rome.

The singing began to subside. Preparations were being made for the *Havdallah* ceremony: the burning of a candle and the inhaling of spices to conclude the Sabbath, to bid farewell to the Sabbath Bride—in Warsaw.

"In California we sing of the swallows that come back to Capistrano each year to mark a holy Catholic feast," I said. "Why did Don Juan Capistrano bring more than his swallow to America? Why did he bring the Inquisition to California? They were burning Jews on the plazas of Mexico as late as 1820."

The priest sighed deeply. Oh, God—I must pull back. I may not dehumanize this priest; not here in the Nozik Shul. His hand is reaching out to mine, here, on the edges of savagery.

I clasped his hand and that of Rav Datner, who had listened to much of what was said. I voiced to each a Hebrew phrase I'd learned long ago: *Hazak v'ematz!* "Be strong and of good courage!"

We walked boldly through deep pools of water that created a passageway of mud—away from the Nozik Shul.

I was determined to join the students on their journey to Majdanek the following morning. To do this, I would have to leave my hotel at 4 a.m.

An awkward hour.

19

How does one sleep in a threadbare, once palatial Hotel Bristol in Warsaw, knowing that somehow I must make it to the railroad station at 4:30 in the morning to join the students on their way to Lublin? And then, to nearby Majdanek.

Lublin: Earl Vinecour describes this city in his book, *Polish Jews, the Final Chapter:* "For Lublin had been the spiritual heart of Polish Jewry, renowned for its schools and sages, one of them so great that he was referred to as the Seer of Lublin."

My friend Israel Eisenberg remembers Lublin in sadness and in horror. He was one of thousands who were shot by the German and hurled into a vast ditch outside the city—the wounded and the dead covered by layers of earth, and more victims hurled upon the heaving mounds.

Israel's bullet grazed his head, leaving an ugly scar.

In the darkness he crawled out of the death cavern and escaped to the woods. Many Germans were to know the wrath of Israel Eisenberg.

These thoughts surge through me as I make my way in the

darkness of the Bristol Hotel to the lobby floor. I ask the desk attendant for help in finding a taxi to the Central Train Station. In the rainflecked Warsaw night, an occasional taxi would hear the attendant's call, only to drive away swiftly.

"Hooligans!" he cried to one driver. Apparently that outburst worked. The driver stopped his taxi, turned it around and picked me up.

At the train station: how to find which of the many ticket windows a clerk might sell me a ticket to Lublin? And which of many platforms would be the right one for the Lublin train? And where were the students?

Despite the early hour, the station was alive with travelers. I found one woman who spoke enough English to direct me to the proper window and then to the proper platform.

There, sleepy and exhausted, were the students, slouched over travel packs or suitcases.

It occurred to me that these youngsters were taking along all their possessions—leaving Warsaw, now, for other memories. The journey to Lublin and Majdanek was to be one of several places to visit. Auschwitz would be last, before their departure for Israel.

A disheveled second-class train pulled up and the students pounced into action. Some rushed into one of the cars, lowered the windows, while others hurled luggage up to them in spectacular rhythm.

We all climbed into the car. Once inside the train, the students fell asleep in their tracks: on seats, in the aisles. Totally out.

In the adjoining car, I found a spot beside a snoring Pole. It hardly mattered, for soon I also was asleep.

But at the instant of dawn, I was awakened by half a dozen of the boys who were putting on prayer shawls and donning *tfillin* in preparation for morning prayers. Here, on a train in Poland headed for Lublin!

The scene was startling—and quite other-worldly for Polish

travelers aboard. The older ones remembered the days of Jewish life in Poland. The younger ones had never seen a Jew in Judenrein Poland.

The singular prayer of the Jew, the *Sh'ma,* was exclaimed in loud voice by the boy *daveners*: "Hear oh Israel, the Lord Our God, the Lord is One!"

Once the prayer was recited everywhere in Poland. Then, only in the camps of infamy and death. Later, not at all.

Now boldly, openly, on the second-class train from Warsaw to Lublin, by Jewish boys on their way to Israel to study.

No one among the many older Poles aboard the train dared to snicker. *Zhid* was an unheard word of derision now. A Holocaust and perhaps an unuttered national guilt had made these prayers aboard a train to an infamous death camp correct, natural, proper. Then, the thought that Israel had already proved the manhood of these boys, now in Jewish prayer aboard a train grinding sadly through a Polish countryside at dawn.

The prayers ended, the prayer shawls folded, the leather thongs of the *tfillin* carefully and lovingly tied—all put away by the boys into pockets of their backpacks. The boys sank into their seats and returned to sleep.

As we all did.

Only to be awakened again by a gnashing of wheels and a stop at a tiny village depot.

A conductor raced through to inform us that this train would not go on to Lublin after all; that those of us who were headed for Lublin would have to get off, cross several tracks with our gear and await another train. Would it be long in coming? Who knows? But this train would be leaving in about one minute. Which meant a magnificent scramble to have the car windows lowered while boys on the train tossed backpacks, suitcases, food parcels down to waiting hands. It appeared to be a mad melee, but obviously these young people were now skilled at this. An amazing operation to watch.

Each item was carefully checked and as the final "OK" was given, the train pulled out. One minute flat.

Our caravan of young people and two old folks, Mrs. Rosen and myself, somehow slithered over a number of tracks to a platform about a thousand yards away and no one knew when the second train to Lublin might arrive.

But to the surprise of everyone, a distant sound was heard from the west and in minutes the train was here. And the loading process began, each according to his or her strength, each according to his or her will.

Within the minute we were all aboard, headed for heart-break.

At Lublin a bus had been arranged to take the group to a youth hostel. I went along and in the lobby of the hostel while the students and Mrs. Rosen were assigned to rooms, my mind relived these ordinary, yet extraordinary events.

The group came down munching apples. Then, as a unit, we walked to a Lublin bus stop. Was it possible that Majdanek could be reached by a city bus in Lublin?

Over the years I had conjured Lublin to be a large Jewish *shtetl*—a bit more than a village. Indeed, I was prepared to scan the roofs of Lublin for the fiddlers or magicians. Would they play a bit louder, so I might compose new lyrics to their song? Would the magic be joyful? I hadn't counted on finding myself in the heart of a large Polish city. Bring on the Jews. Where are the Jews?

Lublin . . . Lublin . . . Lublin . . . a city of sages and not a few Jewish artisans, tailors. Earl Vinecour writes that "nowhere else in the world had there been a *yeshiva* like that of Yeshivat Chachmei Lublin [Academy of the Sages of Lublin].

"So important in the life of the entire Polish nation had been the influence of the great Yeshiva of Lublin, that for centuries its rector was appointed by none other than the King of Poland himself."

When the new, six-story headquarters for the Yeshiva was

dedicated in 1930, Vinecour points out that 50,000 people attended the event, including notables of government. It housed a huge auditorium and scale model of the Temple in Jerusalem. Nine years later, the school's 500 students faced the decimation that consumed other Jews of Poland.

Vinecour cites a horrendous account of German vandalism of the Yeshiva, in the February, 1940 edition of *Deutsche Jugendzeitung*:

"It was a matter of special pride to us to destroy this Talmudic Academy, known as the greatest in Poland. We threw out of the building the large Talmudic library and brought it to the marketplace. There, we kindled a fire under the books. The conflagration lasted twenty hours. The Jews of Lublin stood around, weeping bitterly. Their outcries rose above our own voices. We summoned a military band and the triumphant cries of the soldiers drowned out the noise of the wailing Jews."

Vinecour says there are only 30 Jews left in Lublin out of a population of 46,000 who lived there before Hitlerian tanks brought German *Kultur* to the city. Forty per cent of the total population, then, was Jewish.

*   *   *

Our group of students huddled tightly on the tilting, weaving bus, which brought us directly to the gates of Majdanek.

Dominating the hills and fields in all directions on the edges of Lublin is a massive monument to the victims of Majdanek. It is a structure of free-formed stone—giving off an eerie feeling of a six-branched candelabrum. Six branches of stone, a candle a million.

Sculptor Wiktor Tolkin's work is called by the Polish government "The Monument of Struggle and Martyrdom." The government neglects to say that of the 360,000 victims to perish at Majdanek—most were Jews.

20

There are a number of Lublin bus routes to the eastern edge of the city. Many visitors come to Majdanek by taxi. Some stroll the pleasant countryside—lovers, arm-in-arm.

But a guide at Majdanek reminds the visitor that box cars would arrive at the Lublin central station with macabre regularity from all parts of Europe—the Eichmann Express. The rust-painted freight cars were all sealed and a cargo of humanity was pounding at the walls, pleading for air and water. Each car had its internal cemetery section and heaps of human waste.

No city buses awaited these railroad passengers.

There were savage yells by German soldiers for the victims to get off. There were wild beatings—and always the caravan of death was forced into a stern and rapid walk to Majdanek. Snow, rain, icy roads—children. It hardly mattered.

Those who arrived at Majdanek were stripped of clothing and name and given bizarre prison garb of striped rags—and a tattooed number for a name.

*   *   *

Our small group of Jewish students was led in silence over a wide, rock-paved pathway to the huge monolith memorial, the Homage Road. Nearby is a section of Black Road, which the prisoners traversed on their way to hell.

Once inside the encampment, the guide leads you to a row of barracks on the right; the first, a bathhouse. The German had an obsession with cleanliness that came from waterless shower-heads and smooth stones shaped like soap. This bathhouse was one of seven gas chambers at Majdanek.

Soviet war prisoners were the first to arrive here. Then the hospitality expanded to include Polish political prisoners, and inevitably the Jews. Always, the Jews.

Our students were stoic as they were taken from structure to structure. These are now museums, some describing the various SS plans for the development of Majdanek, others containing the relics of madness: the piles of forelorn shoes, baggage cases, items of humanity where none was to be found in the German eyes.

One building housed sketches and drawings of camp life by artists among the prisoners. One sobs to contemplate the creativity lost. And the children. The children! For them the living and dying conditions were identical with those of the men and women. And the work details told of exhaustive labor from dawn to dusk under the tormenting eyes of German SS or their kapos who manufactured terror with macabre genius.

A section in a pamphlet describing events at Majdanek is revealing:

"A form of mass extermination, employed almost since the first days of the existence of the camp, were executions by shooting, carried out in the camp or in the Krepiecki Wood, seven kilometers away from Majdanek.

"The first mass execution by shooting was carried out on 2,000 Soviet war prisoners in December 1941, while the most atrocious one in the whole history of Majdanek camp was the one carried out on November 3, 1943. 'I had never thought,' wrote Dr. Jan Nowak, a prisoner of the camp, 'that one day I would witness what may be called a superhuman shock.

" 'On November 3rd (and it is only now that I can write about it) since early morning, columns of prisoners were being brought up—Jews, as it proved—and in ditches they were all murdered by shooting from machine guns.

" 'And the loudspeaker on the high pole was sending out foxtrot music, the report of the guns mixing with the sound of the music. It was a dreary November day. The camp was surrounded by triple rows of SS men and from each of the sentry towers, three barrels of machine guns were ready to shoot. They have driven us to the neighboring field IV. Thus, over 18,000 Jews were murdered.' "

All the while, between May and August of 1943 large transports arrived with Jews from the ghettoes of Warsaw and Bialystok. These victims were gassed and the crematoria at Majdanek, one with a Mercedes Benz emblem, became part of the manufacturing process of a super-Aryan race on earth.

*   *   *

Our group was joined by a contingent of young Polish army officers. Some were ashen-faced as they wandered from display to display. We were told that all Polish officers must visit the death camps, especially the huge mausoleum there with its inscription: "Let our fate be a warning to you!"

It became evident that I would have to go on ahead of my young friends and Mrs. Rosen because my train back to Warsaw would leave Lublin at 3 p.m. and I wanted to recite a prayer at the huge crematorium a considerable distance away. I embraced one girl and Mrs. Rosen and I exchanged glances of sorrow with the students which the writing of history will never fathom. I hurried away to the giant crematorium.

There in semi-darkness stood a group of Polish officers. If they had never before heard the Hebrew *Kaddish*, they heard it now.

With each word, my voice reverberated through the chamber of death. The Polish officers watched, immobile. I turned and walked past them into the summer air.

Then down a long, lonely road back to the monument of sorrows and through its archway to the adjoining highway.

Which I crossed to a bus stop. In time, Bus No. 30 came along to take me to the train station.

Lublin.

There are no fiddlers playing upon her roofs.

And I found no magicians.

21

There is a compulsion, here in Poland, to arise at dawn. There is so much to reclaim of a people's thousand-year history in Poland. And there is so little time. Each fragment of memory here is staggering.

Taxi to the Jewish cemetery in Warsaw.

One sees more live Jews at the Jewish cemetery than at any other place in Poland. But they are in reality only a handful and the dead, here, at this unusual burial ground of the Grand Diaspora, are counted in the hundreds of thousands.

A jungle of brush has taken hold and the great cemetery which comforts the remains of writers, historians, scientists — scholars of every discipline of the mind—is a shambles in disarray. Vandals come in the night to plunder the graves, searching for Jewish gold.

The Jewish gold was lost within the lives of these unhonored dead.

Everywhere one comes upon walls that are constructed of broken gravestones. And there are markers on graves without bodies. They were among the millions that went up in smoke.

I go searching for the most famous monument of all in the Warsaw Jewish Cemetery: that of the celebrated Yiddish writer I. L. Peretz, Jacob Dinesohn (novelist) and S. Ansky, author of *The Dybbuk*. It is a literary pantheon, and I must find it.

I search in silence, scanning the names on headstones, tearing my way through weeds that clog the pathways. I walk deep into the shadows. Toppled headstones form contorted images and patterns and it seems that the very earth is beginning to devour the tragedies that befell us.

Steel fences around affluent family plots are rusting into futility. Here, who will come to recite the annual prayers for the dead? Children and grandchildren were consumed by the Holocaust—and who will pray their prayers?

The headstones tell a startling story of people in an unwelcoming land. Here a doctor, here a professor of literature, a historian, a pharmacist. A famous Warsaw mortician could not escape the death wrath of the German.

Here I will light a candle brought from Israel. I have difficulty keeping the flame alive because a low breeze filters swiftly through the underbrush. The flame goes out—but that is hardly an unexpected experience, here, in Warsaw. I must shelter the candle in the sand beside a toppled headstone; then turning, turning, my eyes scan a thousand headstones. I recite the *Kaddish.*

I cannot select one grave to which I may recite the *Kaddish* symbolically. Selection was a German invention.

Then, miraculously, two Jews come upon each other deep within this *Beth Olam,* this House of Eternity. I find a man wandering through the brush even as I am. Searching. He is about 60, erect, wearing a business suit. His eyes light up as I explain my mission—to find the Peretz-Dinesohn-Ansky monument. In Yiddish he says he will take me there.

Afterward, he will take me to the graves of his family. His father was Motel Pinkiert, the famous Warsaw mortician. My new friend is Josef Pinkiert, here to recite Kaddish at the grave-site of his mother, Luba.

We pass the marker over the grave of Zamenhof, inventor of Esperanto, the international language. And we halt for a moment before the marker of Esther Kaminska, founder of the Kaminska Yiddish Theater in Warsaw. Her daughter, Ida Kaminska, fled Poland only a few years ago. She won acclaim as the star of *House on Main Street,* one of the unusual films of the post-war era.

At the writers' memorial I lower my head in tribute: for there have been giants of literature among all peoples in history. These were three of mine. We walk away.

As we walk, Josef tells me that his mother was shot to death on this Hebrew date, in 1942. His uncle, Moses Pinkiert, was also shot at the same time, and by cart they were brought for burial to this cemetery.

Suddenly the uncle came to life, breathing deeply. With medical attention his life might be saved. But a German Gestapo man is there, points a pistol at the uncle's head and an explosion of death rips the cemetery.

Nearby is the Felix Pinkiert family plot. Another uncle. Felix, his wife Roza and their two children were shot to death in the ghetto. Also slain in the Warsaw Ghetto was another uncle, Noah Pinkiert, his wife Sabina, their children Irene and Ruth. And another uncle, Ber Pinkiert, his wife Regina and their son, Sam.

Murdered elsewhere was Esther Pinkiert (an aunt, at Treblinka); Anna Pinkiert Grynstein (aunt) and her husband, Benjamin. And their two children, Ruth and Henry.

There is a marker for Bela Pinkiert, Josef's wife. There is no body under her headstone. There are markers for his daughters, Henia and Rachel. Only markers.

Thus the litany of death for a single Jewish family.

Josef's shoulders shudder as tears roll down his cheeks. My arm is around him. We trudge out of the cemetery and to the side where Josef leads me to his car. He tells me that his home is now in Radom. He lives on a government pension. He reaches into the rear compartment of his car and pulls out a plastic sack from which he takes out a vodka bottle. The bottle contains about 40 or 50 tight rolls of paper.

"A Polish man gave this to me to bring to the Jewish Historical Museum in Warsaw," says Josef. "He found it under a lot of bushes at Austrovia-Shventokshisky [near Kielce, a famous Jewish city]. He thought it is valuable."

Josef says that he had opened one of the tiny scrolls, all about five inches across, but was unable to read the Yiddish. His ability to read Yiddish is limited—as is mine.

He offers to drive me to my hotel but I insist the vodka bottle must be taken at once to the Jewish museum. A treasure? We wave farewell outside the Jewish Cemetery of Warsaw. I find a bus to take me to the Bristol Hotel.

□□□**22**□□□

The newsman, on the firing lines of history, is always under blazing guns of turbulence.

Thus it was in December of 1961 that I found myself in Moscow as a "tourist" but actually there to check out, to the best of my ability, a number of rumors that sifted from the Soviet Union that Jewish life there was endangered. My informant: Adolph Held of the Jewish Labor Committee. Indeed, Held earlier had provided clear evidence of the murders of Yiddish writers and poets in Moscow's Lubianka Prison.

That report was republished broadly in America by other Jewish weeklies besides *Heritage* and the New York Yiddish press. Which prompted the Communist Yiddish paper in New York, the *Freiheit,* to publish a front page blast: "What can that little newpaper on the West Coast know what is going on in the Soviet Union?"

However, within weeks the *Folks-Sztyme* of Warsaw (as noted earlier), successor publication to the internationally famed Yiddish daily, *Haint* (which published Psalms as its requiem three weeks after the German invasion of Poland), printed the now-famous "Cult of the Personality" speech by Nikita Khrushchev—in which the murders of the Jewish writers under Stalin's order was admitted.

A few weeks later Howard Fast quit the Communist Party in America in one of the remarkable testaments of faith ever to appear in print—a document published by *New Masses.*

*   *   *

I visited Jewish homes and spoke with numerous Jews in and about the Moscow Synagogue. All came up with startling disclosures of the destruction of Jewish life in the Soviet Union.

"Shrai gevaldt!" they begged me—when I return to America. "Holler like hell!"

It was with this as backdrop that an Intourist representative suddenly suggested that I might want to meet with a Mr. Aron Vergelis, editor of the Yiddish language magazine, *Sovietsche Heimland,* at his office not far from Red Square.

I had wanted to meet Vergelis, but my sessions with Jewish families were more important. It became clear that Vergelis, also, wanted to meet with me. And so we met. Inside his fortress office with huge steel bars to lock the door.

Vergelis tried to impress me that a new climate of intellectual freedom was evident in Russia. "And, don't you have anti-Semitism in America?" he asked.

(I kept wondering how Vergelis survived the Stalin purge of Yiddish writers. A few years later, Josef Kerler, a Yiddish poet, who was released from years of prison at hard labor in a coal mine in the frozen north, came to Los Angeles. "Vergelis betrayed me to the secret police," said Kerler, bitterly. "He betrayed many others.")

Leaving Moscow, I headed for Israel, where I was met before dawn at the airport by a government car and taken directly to the Jerusalem office of David Ben-Gurion, prime minister of the

Jewish State. There, my senior associate editor, Tom Tugend, was present as I detailed for an hour and a half my Moscow findings to the prime minister. He took down his notes by hand, in Hebrew. (Ben-Gurion always listed his profession as "journalist.")

"What you are telling me will one day become the most important factor in the life of our people. There are three million Jews in Russia today," said Ben-Gurion solemnly.

A few years later, Elie Wiesel wrote his incredible *Jews of Silence* and the lid was blown on the Soviet terror state. Perhaps for all time.

* * *

There may one day again be great, independent Jewish newspapers in the tradition of Warsaw's *Haint* (Today). But there are none upon the world scene, yet.

Haint published two editions daily, read by millions throughout the world, including David Ben-Gurion.

Its successor Yiddish newspaper in Poland, the *Folks-Sztyme,* attempted at first to present a free and independent viewpoint. Earl Vinecour notes that *Folks-Sztyme* went "so far as to criticize the Soviet Union for being the main source of contemporary anti-Semitism."

This all changed in 1967, following the miraculous Israeli victory over combined Arab forces with arms supplied by the Soviet Union.

Poland broke relations with Israel when Russia led the way.

A sudden rage of anti-Semitism swept Poland in 1968 and an estimated 17,000 Jews were driven out of Poland. Only four or five thousand remain.

Samuel Tenenblatt, married to a non-Jew (his children speak no Yiddish) remained to become editor of the now government-subsidized Yiddish *Folks-Sztyme.* He told me, in his rather austere office, that he was a secular Jew, a

Communist—but his heart is with the survival of Israel. "Our only hope," he said.

I told him of my meeting with Aron Vergelis in Moscow. His face froze briefly—then he said for me to call him "Shmuel."

"The Germans left us only with memories and a frightful cemetery," he said. "They killed our Jewish intelligentsia and today we don't have Yiddish writers. There are few who admit to being Jewish. There must be as many as 10,000 assimilated Jews here. It is difficult to obtain statistics. Some are coming back as Jews and even to Jewish traditions such as Seders, Purim, and so on.

"We have a culture center for the Jews. We have the Yiddish theater in this building. The Farband has fourteen clubs in Poland. But on the Holy Days, Jews have no place to go. There isn't a rabbi in the whole country.

"Yes, there were once twenty-seven Yiddish dailies in Poland and more than a hundred weeklies," he said.

I told Shmuel that there were only two Yiddish dailies left in America, several Yiddish weeklies—and about 75 English language weeklies (including the four *Heritage* publications).

But there are a multitude of excellent Jewish periodical and book publications in America—and then, in England, the greatest English language weekly of them all, the *Jewish Chronicle,* is setting high standards.

"It is a problem," said Shmuel Tenenblatt. "A heavy problem. We have no generation to give birth to children. Will our paper end after my time as editor?"

His paper walks a tightrope each week. It contains a smattering of Communist politics, Jewish culture of the past, brief reports about Jews of the world and very short news items. A Polish section is offered to Jews who are unable to read Yiddish.

About anti-Semitism in Poland: he admits there was indeed an anti-Semitic intent to drive all Jews out of Poland. That took place long before Hitler. But nobody thought of Polish anti-Semitism in terms of the physical destruction of a people.

"It's a paradox," he says. "There were no pogroms in Poland. But they happened in Russia. And when Hitler came, many Poles did save Jews.

"Many more might have, but didn't," he sighed.

"Will Jewish life survive in a Poland that contains an Auschwitz?" I asked.

"I can't answer as to how many Jews will be here tomorrow. We have too many old people. I am not too much of an optimist here. I am optimistic about Israel."

I returned the conversation to Aron Vergelis of Moscow.

"Vergelis could put out a good publication, given his resources." Then, again he fell silent.

About Israel: "I am a Jew. The Sabra is Jewish. There will come a healthy nation out of it. But we must think of Jewishness in all the other lands, also. My fatherland is Poland, but my heart is for peace in Israel."

23

Leaving the offices of the *Folks-Sztyme,* I descend a flight of stairs to the lobby of the new Yiddish State Theater, an elegant theater that is successor to the Kaminska Yiddish Theater.

It is a showplace in irony for a Communist government that had virtually completed the job of Hitler by driving out all but about 4,000 Jews from Poland.

This is a Yiddish theater playing to mostly Gentile audiences that speak no Yiddish but listen to translations, via earphones, of the words of actors, many of whom actually know no Yiddish except the few Polish accented sounds they were taught.

The Ansky play, *The Dybbuk,* is still most popular here. Jews are portrayed as bizarre characters of a contorted age ago—and Catholic actors play as rabbis, exorcizing the devil out of Polish actresses playing Jewish women. Vinecour notes that the only "rabbis" in Poland today are Catholics.

In the lobby are three Jewish "Jewish" actors. They are there to prepare programs for the weeks ahead. Alas, I had come during a holiday period and the stage would be dark for several weeks.

The actors are Mendel Bram, Herman Lercher and Moshe Szwejlich. They have many questions to ask: the state of Yiddish in America (a disaster); is there a vital Yiddish theater anywhere in the United States (hardly); then why point the finger at us?

Who is pointing a finger? I tell them we are all playing games. Our children are learning the arts of assimilation, as though Hitler never happened. But you play games—you impress nobody.

One of the actors offers to lead me to the Jewish Historical Institute, to which Josef Pinkiert had gone with his vodka bottle filled with the tiny Yiddish scrolls. I must find out about them.

I am told at the Institute that the vodka bottle had been left with an attendant and there was no one in authority, yet, to have examined them. Perhaps later, if I'll come back. But my train leaves for Konin in the morning. I may never find out.

But I do meet with Dr. Zygmunt Hoffman, assistant director of the museum. There is an unusual display now of sculpture and paintings concerning the Holocaust. Would I care to see it?

He is fearful to mention that the Institute houses 60,000 volumes of Judaica, one of the greatest collections of writings on Jewish subjects and by Jewish authors to be found anywhere. I remind him that thirteen years earlier, before the 1968 outrages by the Polish government, Beryl Mark, the Institute's scholarly director, had taken me through the archives. I had just come from Israel with a personal message of courage for Prof. Mark from President Zalman Shazar. Prof. Mark was entrusted with an enormous treasure. "A good man," said the President.

Prof. Mark showed me the rare manuscripts, one a thousand years old by a Jewish traveler, Eldad HaDani; and the archives of Emanuel Ringelblum—a diary which was discovered after the days of horror, sealed in cans; a great source of facts that became the Warsaw Ghetto history.

Who visits this vast treasure house of Jewish history?

Dr. Hoffman says about 100 persons come each week. Until October 1, 1978, the Polish authorities would allow no books, photographs nor original artifacts of the Holocaust to be sent abroad on exhibition. On that date, at Catholic University's Mullen Library, in Washington D.C., a large quantity of Jewish treasures was placed on display—on loan from the Jewish Historical Institute under auspices of Father Waclaw Zajacz-kowski.

It was the same priest with whom I held a melancholy dialogue on a Saturday night in Warsaw, while American youngsters sang their hearts out in prayer.

The kindly priest, in a subsequent communication to me, said that during the war years he had served as a liaison to the Primate of Poland, August Cardinal Hlond, then in Rome, and that the Polish priests were among the first to confirm the death throes of the Jews in Poland, and to cry out. But he cited only one such statement that was carried by the Polish Catholic Press Agency which declared:

"We are filled with compassion, horror and indignation. God who forbade murder, bids us to protest. Our Christian conscience bids us to protest."

But Vinecour writes about the church in 1968:

"Poland's Cardinal Hlond did not publicly alter his stand, held since 1936, of accusing Jews of sponsoring atheism and Bolshevism in Poland. Thus, the church hierarchy remained deafeningly silent during this (1968) period, as it had during the Nazi Holocaust."

Question.

How was it possible for Father Zajaczkowski to obtain so valuable an exhibition for Catholic University in Washington D.C.?

What will happen to the archives in Warsaw when the elderly Jewish archivists leave the scene? There are only two Jewish archivists at the Institute. Others are not Jewish.

"What will happen after we leave?" asks Dr. Hoffman. "Who knows? We have no youth."

Until the government outrages in 1967 and 1968, there

were 27 Jewish schools in Poland. (In pre-Hitler times, there were thousands.) Now there are no Jewish schools in the land.

Come, he said, leading me to the exhibition of Holocaust art.

First we come upon a painting of the hero of the Ghetto Uprising, Mordechai Anielewicz, done after the war, and a heroic painting of a Jewish fighter with his rifle (there were so few rifles in the Ghetto!), painted by W. Zakrewski.

There was a moving sculpture of a Ghetto fighter, a mother and child, done by Alina Szapocznkow.

And then I was startled to come upon a bronze work by Henryk Glicenstein. Dr. Hoffman called it "The Sorrowing Messiah."

"The original is in the Vatican," he said.

Glicenstein was an important sculptor in Israel until his death in New York—hit by a taxi. The piece is actually "The Sorrowing Moses," I told Dr. Hoffman. Henryk Glicenstein was my father's cousin. There is a Glicenstein Museum in Sfad, Israel.

A young man from Britain comes to visit. He speaks English and Hebrew. Dr. Hoffman speaks Polish and German. The Yiddish actor, who had accompanied me to the Institute, had served as interpreter for me, speaks no Hebrew. Now he must leave. I join as the archivist leads the British student through the exhibition. There is no verbal communication.

Esperanto, the universal language invented by Zamenhof, might have helped. But Zamenhof lies buried in the Jewish cemetery nearby.

I was told by my actor friend the direction to the Warsaw Ghetto monument, now situated on a postage stamp area. All that is left to remind the world that the Warsaw Ghetto once covered almost a third of the entire city.

Thirteen years ago much of the Ghetto was still largely a wasteland, although high-rise apartment buildings were beginning to be rooted in the turbulent, scream-encrusted soil.

24

This section of Warsaw—this grisly section of earth with its modern high-rise apartment buildings, its Polish street names, its Polish children playing in the parkways and Polish mothers wheeling carriages while themselves again grown with child— once contained 600,000 Jews packed by madness, tortured by hunger. And before the apartment complexes rose, heroism became rooted here; and whenever national heroism will ever again be measured it will be against a human will that had a handful of men, women and children hurling rocks at the power of German arms.

The Ghetto Warsaw was reduced to rubble, but the ragtag fighters led by Mordechai Anielewicz fought longer against the German than did Poland—indeed, than did France when the "Phoney War" ended and the German thrust began toward Dunkirk.

And when the Ghetto was demolished in fire and flame, *Götterdämmerung* had begun for Adolf Hitler. And Himmler. And Goering. And Goebbels. And Adolph Eichmann whom I watched for weeks behind his cage of glass in Jerusalem, an animal begging a Jewish nation for mercy.

There are a few Jewish names on streets where once the Ghetto stood in Warsaw: Anielewicz Street; Zamenhof Street.

Where these streets converge one finds the Warsaw Ghetto Memorial—a 36-foot bronze statue of a struggling people fighting to Sanctify the Name, created by Nathan Rapaport. In front of the monument is a huge Menorah, protected by two Lions of Judah. Behind the monument is a granite wall made of stone blocks sent to Warsaw by the German for a monument to be erected in celebration of Hitler's victory over the Jews.

In front of the monument is a small plaza—and apartment complexes in all directions.

Do they sleep at nights, these Polish families, living among the screams that once inhabited these fields?

Before the German came, Warsaw was the cultural center of Jewish life on earth. It was teeming with art and artistry; music, theater, poetry. An uncanny trade and manufacturing center. A society of Jews had given a Golden Age to a Poland that for the most part envied them and listened to the poison of priests, turning a deaf ear to the warnings of priests of compassion who could not really be heard.

I'd been there before, but I must find the bunker that had once stood at Mila 18 and from which Anielewicz had organized the Uprising. The bunker had been moved half a mile from Mila 18—which was expropriated as the site of yet another apartment building.

One searches in vain to see even a fragment of the high brick wall the Jews were forced to erect in order to complete their entrapment. I wonder as I scan the tall Ghetto Monument what whim it would take for the Polish government to order the destruction of the heroic figures on the monument. And to eliminate the Jewish names on the street signs.

The bunker is now grass-covered, trim, well-attended in a parklike setting surrounded by a small steel fence, with bushes at its sides. Atop the former Ghetto nerve center is a rough stone with engraved Yiddish writing telling of the heroism of the Jewish fighters "for freedom and the honor of Poland."

Poland had little to do with the savagery of the fight put up by the Ghetto Jews. There was none to join them from the Aryan side when the chips were down.

Father Zajaczkowski asked me, that Sabbath night at the Nozik Synagogue: "Who are the heroes?"

The heroes are all about me, here, as I stand on the bunker that once stood bravely at Mila 18. And they are Jewish. All of them Jewish!

Suddenly, from out of the darkened bushes to my side I hear a "rat-tat-tat" of boys firing make-believe machine guns, playing at soldiers.

They had thrust small tubes through holes cut through cardboard boxes. These Polish children were now the Jewish fighters.

Their grandparents were not there to help. Indeed, it is hardly unkind to suggest that for the most part the word *Zhid* was on a nation's tongue — even when attacked by Hitler; even as Jews fought bravely in the Polish army for Polish freedom.

But the boys are beautiful. One, wearing glasses, smiles out of his bunker at me. He has a sensitive face. A child is a child.

I recite the *Kaddish* softly atop the bunker.

It starts to rain. I rush for a taxi.

Tomorrow I must make a pilgrimage to Konin, the birth-place of my father.

25

Konin was also the birthplace of Michael Goldwasser, the grandfather of Barry Goldwater.

Michael Goldwasser must have grown up knowing my grandfather, Julian Dobrzinsky, who became a celebrated chess player in Central Europe.

But getting to Konin would tax a sardine's penchant for intimacy. I was told to wait for the train at Peron 1 (platform 1) only to learn that the section for Konin was way down the platform—almost beyond reach as a rampaging throng began charging to get aboard the train.

I notice two nuns being tossed aboard one of the cars. They are flustered by the indignities and it's all a big joke to the shoving passengers.

A young man grabs one of my bags when I ask directions to the Konin car. I carry another bag and a parcel and we storm forward. Would the train leave us? A distinct possibility. It was bedlam. At last, an open platform on the Konin section of the train and the young man and I climb aboard. Dozens of others follow and within seconds a pall of smoke fills the platform area of the train. Forget trying for a seat. A window ledge sticks out two inches—that's my seat to Konin. At least, on this train.

The young man tells me in his broken German (which I manage to translate into my shattered Yiddish) that he is an electrical engineer. He grimaces as the train passes a Russian military camp with its inevitable idealized portrait of Lenin. He loves his Poland, he says, but cannot stomach the Russians who have become an occupying force in his country.

Two and a half hours of jostling, foul cigarette smoke, hacking coughs and the train approaches Konin. The young man helps again, carries one of my bags to a waiting taxi. "To the Konin Hotel," I tell the driver. The meter reads 8 zlotys. I pay him. It is midafternoon and I decide to take a bus ride into the old town of Konin which adjoins the new section with its hotels and huge apartment buildings.

My father would often tell me of his native Konin, the tiny *shtetl* of Jews not very far from the German border city of Poznan. Our family had long ago established a mill on a rather large estate. They became pillars of the Konin Synagogue and the *yeshiva* which my father attended. As one of Konin's most prominent families, a large section of the Jewish cemetery was given over to the Dobrzinsky plot.

I had been to Konin in 1962, traveling by car from Warsaw.

The new section had not yet been started. I had called on the police chief for help in finding a single Jew in Konin. The chief laughed: *"Hitler geschossen alle Juden."*

Big joke. Indeed, it was true. Jews were lined up in the town square, 10,000 of them, and massacred. None escaped. My family among the victims.

I get off the bus in Old Konin and walk slowly about the town square. Where did my cousins stand in the final moments? Or other relatives?

I cross over to the town library. This was once the *yeshiva*, the Jewish school which my father attended. I am allowed inside, greeted by an American song on the library music system: "Love Is a Many Splendored Thing." Even here, in Konin! But alas, too late.

The song is sung in French. That hardly matters. An attendant tells me that this section of the library was once the office of the rabbi. And the adjoining building was the Synagogue itself, with its four center pillars that held up the roof and a marvelous array of frescoes on the walls.

The walls are boarded, but I notice Hebrew inscriptions above the doorway. I pull the double doors apart a bit for a better view inside. The sanctuary is now a warehouse for sacks of flour and construction material.

It is becoming twilight, dark and gray. I board a bus to take me to my hotel, passing the town square again with its frightful memories. The square seems smaller now than when I was here the first time. On the earlier visit, the square was blanketed with snow and women were carrying pails of water hanging from halters about their necks. The water came from hand pumps in the square.

The intervening years brought dramatic changes to Konin—cinemas, taxis, supermarkets. On the bus ride back to my hotel, a hostile Polish man pushes his face close to mine, muttering words in drunken gibberish. I try to placate him. He edges toward the door and at a bus stop, gets off, angrily gesturing to me to get off. I ignore him and the bus proceeds. Drops me off in front of the Konin Hotel.

"Since they came," a voice says, "we've had nothing but trouble."

It was an older woman who had gotten off the bus with me.

No, she hadn't heard of my family. She'd come to Konin after the war. Now she was bitter about the Russians. But she recalled that many Jewish friends had perished at the hands of Hitler. Her best girl friend had fled to Palestine, to safety.

She's a tiny woman, overwhelmed by events which her eyes recall. She wanted me to know the horrors she felt during the days of the German occupation. And now the Russians. She accompanies me to my hotel, then walks on alone to her flat, with her thoughts.

It is still midsummer but my room in Konin is bitterly cold: distant, cold and sorrowful. Tomorrow I must search for the Jewish cemetery. At least finding the names of Jewish families on headstones—a chasm of sorts might be bridged.

The next morning, by bus back to the Old Town. It occurred to me that my father had celebrated his Bar Mitzvah at the Konin Synagogue. What happened to the Torah scrolls? Steel bars crisscross the broken windows. Was the Synagogue used by the German as a holding prison for the Jews of Konin? I glance through the doors again and notice the elegance of architecture; the separate balcony for women. Did my grandmother pray from this balcony? The smell of freshly baked bread and cakes permeates the abandoned Synagogue complex.

I inquire of a number of Konin taxi drivers if they know the way to the Jewish cemetery. There is always someone with a smattering of English. One driver asks a passing woman if she ever heard of a Jewish cemetery in Konin. The talk in Polish is rapidfire. She points in a direction past the Synagogue. The driver takes me to the gates of the Catholic cemetery.

"Jewish cemetery!" I exclaim to the driver.

"Come."

I follow him inside and he points to a short stump of man, the caretaker, who leads me through the cemetery and up a pathway that is slippery with last night's rain, past many Catholic markers and finally, at the crest of a hill, there is a plot marked off by a low iron fence—about fifteen feet wide, a hundred feet long.

In the center of one section of the iron fence is a stone marker containing a Star of David and the words in Polish: *"Bestialsko Zamdrdowanym Zdom Przez Katow Hitlerowskich— w Obozie w Czarkowie w Latach 1941-1943—Rodacy, Konin XI-1945 R."*

"Murders beyond bestiality, committed by Hitlerite killers in Camp of Czarkow in the years 1941 to 1943—Compatriots of Konin, November 1945."

It is the mass burial grave of victims of the Konin massacre.

I had stumbled upon a shrine of Jewish history. What happened in Konin had somehow been erased from human memory. The caretaker is left to remember. He was the grave-digger. Once, he had allowed a Jew to escape and he was a hunted man by the Germans. He fled to Warsaw, to the safety of anonymity.

The grave also contains the body of his brother, he says in halting German.

"My brother helped dig the grave," says the caretaker. "Because he gave some potatoes to three Jews, a Gestapo stomped on the potatoes and machine-gunned my brother and the Jews. This is his grave, too. All of them are here."

The caretaker raises his hands as though holding a machine-gun—and suddenly makes the sounds of the rapid fire of a machine gun. Just as did the boys at Mila 18.

Thousands of bodies are in layers at my feet. Nobody comes in prayer here. "You are the first."

Again a candle from Israel; the *Kaddish* and the *Sh'ma.*

In silence we walk down the pathways of the Catholic cemetery and I wait for a bus to take me to my hotel.

As I get off the bus, directly overhead is a huge, three-sided poster of Lenin. I glance about this new section of Konin. It has a patina of irony, that once, terrible things had happened here.

The faces of Lenin have an awesome effect on the face of Poland.

26

It is still midmorning. If I hurry I might make the train to Poznan and then Breslau (in German), Wroclaw (in Polish).

I must leave Konin at once. I feel a constriction, the chord that tied me to the roots of my family's years in Konin had somehow become a constriction about my throat.

The Poles wanted Poland *Judenrein.*

The German wanted Europe *Judenrein.*

I leave them with their emptiness as I gather mine for the train ride to Breslau. I watch the countryside in silence as the train grinds toward Poznan. They make lousy farmers, these Poles, who managed to keep the Jews off the land and then wanted a piece of the action in the cities.

The farmers of Europe ought to take short courses (no, long courses!) in farming upon the *kibbutzim* of Israel.

It is raining in Poznan, and cold, as I wait on the platform for the train to Breslau. There existed a vital Jewish experience,

once, in Poznan, but I am already numbed by my journey into
savagery. I have a compulsion to leave Poland. I'd had enough.

But Breslau. Wroclaw. There was the Storch Synagogue—
left intact by the German but vandalized by the Poles following
the 1967 Six Day War in the Middle East. Guess the Poles would
place their graffiti marks on history. A brave attack upon an
empty Synagogue shell.

The Synagogue is the central feature of a complex of struc-
tures that once held significant social services for Jews of Lower
Silesia. Most importantly, the buildings housed the historic
Breslau Jewish Theological Seminary, forerunner to America's
large Conservative Movement in Judaism. The vast library of
this Seminary was plundered by the Nazis, placed aboard boxcars and consigned to Germany.

The same boxcars that carried cargoes of Jews on rails of
the Orient Express to the camps of hell.

Somehow, these boxcars were found intact, after the war,
and the books were brought to the Jewish Historical Institute in
Warsaw to form the central core of the great collection of
Judaica there.

Through the soft glisten of rainfall, my taxi heads toward
lodgings at the Monopol Hotel, arranged for me by Orbis, the
Polish tourist service.

This was once an elegant German hotel, much like the
Bristol in Warsaw. Also now threadbare. But also containing a
dance cafe and restaurant. There is a drabness in the dress of
the guests as they arrive for dinner at the Monopol. The orches-
tra plays American music and a girl singer offers her songs in
English—while a mouse scampers atop the edge of the wood
paneling, two-thirds up the sides of the dining hall.

A waiter tries to wave a large napkin to shoo the mouse
away, to no avail. The patrons applaud the mouse. It's all a
game of survival. Life, after all! Even here, in Poland, once
Germany.

It suddenly occurs to me that after World War II the Poles

evicted all the Germans of this city (with authority of the Kremlin)—and a German city became Polish. Wars do have their realities for powerful nations and the dynamics of war bring on the realities called "spoils." Which Wroclaw is.

(But these rules are only for nations such as the Soviet Union and its takeover of vast regions of Finland; the United States and its occupation of Mexico from California to Texas; France, and its hegemony over Alsace-Lorraine. The list is endless. But these rules are not for Israel in the return of the Jewish people to Samaria and Judea—described by forgetful or willful purists as the "West Bank.")

As I pick away at my food, I keep cheering inwardly for the mouse on the restaurant panel. We have a compact in survival, the mouse and I, and I raise a glass of beer to him. (Oh, or her. No matter, indeed.)

In the morning, following a futile visit to the Synagogue complex (there were no Jews to be encountered), I purchase my ticket to Frankfurt, where I would board a British Airways plane to London, thinking my journey was by now over.

But there are overtones, and they follow me relentlessly until I board that plane.

I find myself inside Car 254, a German second-class "wagon" but far classier than Polish first-class. Beside me is a young, bearded American student who had spent the summer in Poland as an exchange student from Florida University. He attended Mickiewicz University in Wroclaw and I tap him for his experiences.

He tells me how Polish students respond on campus to Soviet control of the country. By telling jokes.

Here are samples of the jokes:

A Polish man comes to a magic pond and out leaps a magic fish.

"How do I know that you are a magic fish?" asks the man.

"Try me. I offer to fulfill three of your wishes," saith the fish.

The man promptly says: "For my first wish—I wish that all the Chinese people come to Poland."

"That's odd. What is your second wish?"

"My second wish is that all the Chinese people come to Poland."

The magic fish looks perplexed. "What is your third wish?"

"That all the Chinese people come to Poland."

The fish suddenly asks: "Why the same wish three times?"

"That would have the Chinese cross Russia six times."

*   *   *

Brezhnev and Carter are at Camp David and after the first night there, the Russian leader tells President Carter that he had a dream—"That a strange flag was flying over the Capitol Dome in Washington, all red, with a hammer and sickle on it."

Carter then must have his dream and the following morning at breakfast, the President tells his dream: "I dreamed I saw many banners flying over Red Square and the Kremlin. I was troubled, however, because all the banners contained Chinese writing."

*   *   *

The Palace of Culture dominates the city of Warsaw. It is a replica of the Moscow University building.

According to the Polish students, the only way to see Warsaw is from the top of the Palace of Culture.

That way you won't see the Palace of Culture.

*   *   *

The jokes take on multitudinous flavors. An example:

Jesus, Mohammed and Mayor Daley of Chicago were on a boat.

A storm comes up and Jesus tells his companions, "Oops, there's room on this boat for only one of us."

Mayor Daley says: "Well, then, let's take a vote."

Which Daley wins, 57 to 2.

*   *   *

Night comes swiftly as we approach the East German border. At midnight it will be September 1, 1978. I tell the young American student that it will be the 39th anniversary of the German invasion of Poland which took place on September 1, 1939. Poland had warned Hitler of bitter consequences if he attacked. But Poland collapsed in three weeks.

Armies don't win wars by the excellence of marching in public squares. I recall newsreel films of Polish armies marching in precision. How pathetic the Polish bravado.

It is midnight and our train stops at the border. East German guards promptly inspect the train to make certain that no one ultimately escapes to West Germany from the East. Huge lanterns scan undercarriages of the train. They search the toilet compartments, overhead racks, the space beneath the seats.

I have a sudden urge to yell out: *"Achtung!*March!" It would take only that to have them fall in line.

Yet, the passport control officer is disarmingly friendly and warm. Hardly the tough goon I encountered in Czechoslovakia. I'm sorry that he is so nice. And I despise myself for my feeling of bitterness to a human being.

We are now racing through East Germany. It is far easier, this crossing into East Germany, than when I entered through Checkpoint Charlie several months after the Berlin Wall was erected and John Kennedy exclaimed in West Berlin: *"Ich bin ein Berliner!"*

Through Dresden, where iron heels clicked sharply. And Jews died. Through Leipzig. Through Weimar. I recall something about a Weimar Republic having been established in Germany after the Kaiser fell. I remember the Kaiser hanging in effigy from lampposts on State Street in Chicago the night of the Armistice in 1918.

Crossing into West Germany is a snap for those of us with American passports. The new train conductor must stoop low to enter the compartments. He is about six feet-ten inches tall.

"Play basketball?" I ask. He laughs. We all laugh.

□□□**27**□□□

The train tracks of Germany are inordinately quiet and smooth. There is no rhythmic sound of wheels striking track separations as on the Orient Express run from Istanbul nor the Chopin Express from Vienna to Krakow.

At dawn, I notice great affluence in the countryside of West Germany, in the towns and villages. The homes are as I found them in Austria, beautifully designed with trim landscaping. Suddenly, tall buildings rise up as we enter the mercantile heartland of Germany: Frankfurt. Immense factories are everywhere; traffic is busy to get where it must for the commercial day to begin.

Then, slowly, slowly, the train enters the Frankfurt station. I find a bank window to exchange $10 for German marks. The American dollar is in decline. I receive 17.65 marks for the ten dollars—most of which would go for breakfast and a ticket for the train ride to the Frankfurt airport. I would be out of Germany in a few hours. For me, enough.

I muse aloud to the teller at the bank window: "This is a historic day."

(Everyone now speaks English in Germany. The legacy of Hitler—that the Germans are now very British.)

"Why?" asks the teller.

"The German army crossed into Poland 39 years ago today," I say.

"I wasn't born then," says the teller.

Man in back of me in line says: "Nobody here wants to talk about it." He's traveling through, just as I am.

I load my bags on a station cart and wheel it to the commuter train platform to board a train for the airport.

There, at the airport station, I find another cart, which I wheel to an escalator that would take me to the main lobby of the Frankfurt airport.

I carry one bag and a parcel onto one of two moving stairways going up to the airport lobby.

Two-thirds of the way up, I hear a scream on the escalator to my left—and watch in horror as a woman falls backward on the moving stairway, her suitcase atop her, her feet up forward.

I race to the top of the steps with my parcels, drop them, and dash down the upward staircase, grabbing the suitcase off the woman, then pulling her to her feet.

Had her hair or dress been caught into working of the staircase at the top, she could have been killed. I then race down an adjoining stairway to grab my other parcel, by this time breathless and shaken by the incident.

At the top of the staircase I see the woman is surrounded by her family. I suddenly realize that not one had made an effort to rescue her—two were young men.

She leaves her family, thanking me in rapidfire German. She is as shaken as I. She says I had saved her life and is grateful. Tears roll down her cheeks.

Damned if I don't exclaim in German: "*Ich bin ein Jude! Ich bin ein Jude!*"

A strange and understanding wisp of smile crosses her face.

Rescued by a Jew. She understood it all. She was old enough.

Oh, what the hell!

I dash for the plane to London.

INDEX